THE HISTORY OF
ROCK & ROLL

THE HISTORY OF ROCK & ROLL

David Shirley

FRANKLIN WATTS
A Division of Scholastic Inc.
New York Toronto London Auckland Sydney
Mexico City New Delhi Hong Kong
Danbury, Connecticut

Frontispiece: Bill Haley and the Comets shake, rattle, and roll.

Photographs copyright ©: AP/Wide World Photos: 49, 54, 116, 149; Archive Photos: 82 (Popperfoto), 105 (The Platt Collection), 17, 46, 61, 66, 90; Corbis-Bettmann: 71 (Frank Driggs); Frank Driggs Collection: 10, 26, 37, 79, 96, 111, 123, 140; Retna Ltd: 146 (Jeanette Beckman), 150 (Jay Blakesberg), 138 (Gary Gershoff); UPI/Corbis-Bettmann: 2, 31, 103, 127, 130.

Library of Congress Cataloging-in-Publication Data

Shirley, David, 1955–
The history of rock and roll / David Shirley.
    p. cm.
Includes bibliographical references (p.) and index.
Summary: Traces the history of rock and roll music from the 1950s to the present day and discusses its changing styles and leading personalities.
  ISBN 0-531-11332-9 (lib. bdg.)   ISBN 0-531-15846-2 (pbk)
  1. Rock music—History and criticism—Juvenile literature.
[1. Rock music—History and criticism.] I. Title.
ML3534.S4855   1997
781.66'09—dc20   96-33610
                                                          CIP
                                                       AC MN

CONTENTS

INTRODUCTION

It is the early evening of March 5, 1951. In the back room of a small recording studio in Memphis, Tennessee, five young musicians are setting up their equipment and trading wisecracks. Leaning across his piano, band leader Ike Turner interrupts the small talk to give some last-minute instructions to the band before the taping begins.

Turner and his band specialize in rhythm and blues, the same kind of slow, throbbing tunes played by their friends on the Memphis blues circuit, such as Riley "B. B." King, Rufus "Hound Dog" Thomas Jr., and Herman "Little Junior" Parker. This evening's tune is a little different, however.

Written by the band's baritone saxophone player, Jackie Brenston, the song, "Rocket 88," has a lighter, livelier feel than the band's normal repertoire. As the tape begins to roll, the song kicks off predictably enough, with Willie Sims's light, swishing drums and Willie Kizart's fuzzy guitar churning out a tight, dependable boogie-woogie rhythm. All at once, Turner pounds out a series of hard staccato phrases on his piano keys, and the song suddenly comes to life. As Brenston begins to sing the lyrics—a good-natured tribute to a customized Oldsmobile—you can hear the smile on his face and the gentle bobbing of his head. "Blow your horn, Raymond! Blow!" Brenston shouts to his fellow saxophone player, Raymond Hill, at the end of the second verse. But instead of toning down to make room for Hill's solo, the musicians all play even harder and louder, with Turner thrashing away at his keyboard like a maniac. By the time Brenston and Hill burst into a frenzied duet at the end of the song, Turner's piano has dropped out altogether—perhaps he has collapsed, exhausted, on the floor—and Kizart's distorted rhythm guitar has risen to a steady roar.

All the band members are exhilarated when the taping is finished. Turner, who also works as a talent scout for a couple of blues-oriented record labels, knows at once that the band has done something special. He wonders, however, if there are enough record buyers out there who will also be excited by the band's new explosive style of playing.

In fact, there were more than enough listeners just waiting to hear "Rocket 88" and more songs like it. Released that same April by Chicago's Chess Records, the song quickly rose to the number-one position on the rhythm-and-blues charts. In the meantime, Turner had removed his name from the recording to appease his employers at Modern Records, who were angry that their young talent scout had sold the song to their competitors at Chess. Consequently, "Rocket 88," the first rock-and-roll recording, was not released by the Ike Turner Band but by Jackie Brenston and His Delta Cats.

The following year, a young white disc jockey from Chester, Pennsylvania, named Bill Haley released his own version of "Rocket 88." Haley's version of the song lacked the energy and excitement of the original single, and it failed to attract much attention among record buyers or radio listeners around the country. Haley kept trying, however, and over the next two years, he released several hip finger-snapping singles, including "Rock the Joint," "Crazy, Man, Crazy," "Rock Around the Clock," and "Shake, Rattle and Roll." The last tune, a hard, swinging cover of a blues classic by Big Joe Turner, eventually found its way into the pop singles top ten and even became a minor hit in England.

In the American south, a number of rhythm-and-blues musicians had begun to bring a distinctly southern flavor to Haley's hip, spirited mix of rhythm and blues and country-and-western swing. In 1952, New Orleans musicians Antoine "Fats" Domino (with "Goin' Home") and Lloyd Price (with "Lawdy, Miss Clawdy") both released successful hard-rocking rhythm-and-blues records. The following year, blues shouter Willie Mae Thornton performed a loud, raucous version of Leiber and Stoller's "Hound Dog" for the Johnny Otis Band.

Rock-and-roll music really began to make an impact in 1955, however, when Bill Haley's "Rock Around the Clock" was rereleased as part of the sound track for the popular Hollywood film *The Blackboard Jungle.* The song had already been a modest hit for the singer when it was originally released the year before. With the exposure provided by the film, however, the record rose steadily up the charts to become the first rock-and-roll record to reach number one on the *Billboard* pop singles chart. "Rock Around the Clock" also climbed to number 14 on the rhythm-and-blues charts—the best indication of what young black record buyers wanted to hear. With his gum-smacking, finger-snapping dance music, Haley had finally found a sound that both black and white listeners could enjoy. It proved to be a formula for instant success. By 1956, the former Pennsylvania disc jockey had sold more than three million records.

With the exception of Haley, however, the majority of the

other early rock-and-roll musicians were black. It had been an amazing feat for a white musician like Haley to cross over into the black rhythm-and-blues market with "Rock Around the Clock." Most record executives realized that it would be even more difficult for a black artist to achieve mainstream success with a predominantly white audience. Across the nation, record company owners—such as the Chess brothers in Chicago and young Sam Phillips at Sun Records in Memphis—began looking for white musicians like Haley who could play and sing this exciting new version of rhythm and blues.

Record company owners were not the only people to notice what was happening, however. Around the country, more and more people were beginning to notice the loud, aggressive new form of music—and its enormous appeal for teenagers. One of the earliest champions of rock and roll was New York disc jockey Alan Freed.

Disc jockey Alan Freed introduces a new record on his *Rock 'n' Roll Party* radio show. Disc jockeys at other stations followed Freed's lead, and rock-and-roll fever quickly swept the nation.

A former classical musician with a talent for stirring up controversy, Freed had first become interested in rock and roll while working for the radio station WJW in Cleveland, Ohio, in the early 1950s. By the time he signed with New York's WINS in 1954, he had become a total convert to the new form of music. With the station's support, he organized a number of huge music shows in New York, featuring record-setting crowds and an impressive list of rock-and-roll and rhythm-and-blues standouts, such as Domino, Haley, Hank Ballard, the Orioles, Little Walter, and Muddy Waters. Freed's shows were so successful, in fact, that police sometimes had to be called in to restrain the overexcited young crowds.

"Rock and roll," reported *Life* magazine at the time, "is both music and dance. The music has a rhythm often heavily accented on the second and fourth beat. The dance combines the Lindy and the Charleston [popular dance styles from the 1920s], and almost anything else. In performing it, hollering helps and a boot banging the floor makes it even better. The overall result frequently is frenzy."[1]

By the middle of 1955, rock and roll had clearly found its audience. The problem now was to find more musicians who could play it.

SAM PHILLIPS FINDS HIS STAR

Memphis disc jockey Sam Phillips began recording local blues and rhythm-and-blues musicians in his tiny Sun Studio in 1950. Phillips knew from the beginning that many of the artists who passed through the doors of his studio had something special to offer—a harder, livelier edge to their music that Memphis teenagers found extremely exciting. Among the gifted young musicians whom he recorded during the early 1950s were Herman "Little Junior" Parker, Rufus "Hound Dog" Thomas Jr., Riley "B. B." King, and Chester "Howlin' Wolf" Burnett.

From Thomas's finger-snapping dance tunes to the rough blues shouts of Howlin' Wolf, Phillips's early roster of musicians was remarkably diverse. What all of Phillips's early standouts did share, however, was their race. At a time when mainstream radio play and record sales were dominated by white musicians and white musical styles, the early recording artists at Sun Studio were all black performers. No matter how impressed he was with his young black artists' music, Phillips feared that they would never be able to achieve anything better than modest success on the record charts. Their audience would always be limited, he felt, to the much smaller African-American market. If the new style of music that was now sweeping Memphis and the surrounding area was ever to find a mainstream national audience, it would have to be introduced by a white musician.

"These records appealed to white youngsters," Phillips later said of his early blues and rhythm-and-blues releases, "but there was something in many of those youngsters that resisted buying this music. . . . They liked the music, but they weren't sure whether they ought to like it or not. So I got to thinking how many records you could sell if you could find white performers who could play and sing in this same exciting, alive way."[2]

Late one afternoon during the summer of 1953, Phillips finally found the young white musician he was looking for when 18-year-old Elvis Presley walked timidly through the front door of Sun Studio. Born on January 8, 1935, in the small southern town of Tupelo, Mississippi, Elvis Aron Presley was the only son of Vernon and Gladys Presley. At the time of Elvis's birth, the young couple were struggling financially even by the modest standards of the low-income East Tupelo neighborhood where they lived.

Shy and withdrawn as a child, Elvis displayed an early love for music. By the time he received his first guitar, a gift for his eleventh birthday, he had already performed in a county talent show for children at the local fairgrounds. Singing Red Foley's "Old Shep," a mournful ballad about a boy and his dog, the 10-year-old Presley did not win the contest. But he did take home a fifth-place ribbon, along with a desire to perform in public that would never abandon him. For the next few years, however, the boy's extreme shyness would limit his musical performances to his family, closest friends, and the local Baptist congregation where he sometimes sang in the choir.

"I took the guitar, and I watched people," Presley would

remember years later, "and I learned to play a bit. But I would never sing in public. I was very shy about it, you know."[3]

Although he was usually too timid to share what he was learning, Elvis was already absorbing everything around him—from the slow, stately hymns of his local church to the louder, more frenzied music sung by the black Pentecostal congregations across town. Every Saturday night, Elvis and his parents sat around the radio to listen to the weekly broadcast of the Grand Ole Opry. The country music station provided the young boy with his first exposure to the sad, haunting music of country and bluegrass stars, such as Roy Acuff, Ernest Tubb, and Bill Monroe.

After the family moved 90 miles up the road to Memphis in 1947, Elvis began listening to the hard blues and rhythm and blues played on local radio programs hosted by performers like Sonny Boy Williamson, Howlin' Wolf, Rufus Thomas, and B. B. King. In 1950, Elvis first began hearing recordings produced at Sam Phillips's Sun Studio. Elvis loved Phillips's recordings of artists like Thomas, King, and Little Junior Parker and the Blue Flames. In fact, it was one of Phillips's most recent releases—a sweet ballad called "Just Walkin' in the Rain" by a group of ex-convicts known as the Prisonaires—that inspired Presley to make his first trip to Sun Studio.

Although he was having a hectic day, Phillips listened attentively as Presley recorded two gentle ballads from the 1940s: Jon and Sandra Steele's "My Happiness" and the Ink Spots' "That's When Your Heartaches Begin." Phillips could tell right away that the 18-year-old singer had talent, even on the moody, out-of-date tunes that Elvis had chosen for his informal audition. Before returning to his other duties, Phillips complimented Elvis on his performance, saying that he would probably contact the young singer soon about a recording assignment. Like other studio owners, Phillips often hired local singers and musicians to perform on the records he produced.

Almost a year passed, however, before Phillips offered Presley the chance to record a few tracks with two of his best studio musicians, guitarist Scotty Moore and bass player Bill Black. For months, Moore and Black had been struggling to find the right sound for their country band, the Starlite Wranglers, and Phillips felt that the eager young singer might be the missing ingredient. The three men rehearsed together at the studio for a couple of days with little success, until the evening of July 5, 1954. Exhausted from another full but unproductive day, Phillips and the other musicians were about to call it quits. Suddenly, Presley began singing an old blues song by Arthur "Big Boy" Crudup called "That's All Right (Mama)." Sitting in the recording booth, Phillips knew immediately that he had finally found the sound for which he had been searching—and the young performer to sing it.

"All of a sudden," Scotty Moore would later recall, "Elvis just started singing this song, jumping around and acting the fool, and then Bill picked up his bass, and he started acting the fool, too, and I started playing with them. Sam, I think, had the door to the control booth open—I don't know, he was either editing some tape, or doing something—and he stuck his head out and said, 'What are you doing?' And we said, 'We don't know.' 'Well, back up,' he said, 'try to find a place to start, and do it again.' "[4]

Released two weeks later, along with a light, jangling version of Bill Monroe's "Blue Moon of Kentucky," "That's All Right (Mama)" immediately began to cause a sensation among both white and black listeners in the area. Two months later, Presley, Moore, and Black released an equally popular follow-up single—a hard, bouncy version of Roy Brown's "Good Rockin' Tonight"— Presley's future as a rock-and-roll performer was secure. In less than a year, he became the most popular young entertainer in the mid-south, introducing his new style of music to top country venues like the Louisiana Hayride and the Grand Ole Opry and selling out his own concerts and road shows wherever he went.

By the summer of 1955, Elvis had become so successful that Phillips realized his young star had finally outgrown Sun Records' limited resources. Phillips knew that Presley had the potential to sell far more records than his small business could possibly produce or distribute. Even if he did try to give his talented young star the

A young Elvis wows an audience.

kind of national exposure that he deserved, Phillips would have to neglect the new stable of rockabilly and hard-country artists that he had recently recruited for his label. In light of Elvis's success, Phillips had high hopes for singers Roy Orbison, Carl Perkins, and Johnny Cash, all of whom had recently signed contracts with Sun Records. Perkins, a young rockabilly guitarist with a sound remarkably similar to Presley's, had just recorded a new single called "Blue Suede Shoes" that Phillips felt certain would soon be challenging Elvis's recordings on the charts.

In November 1955, Presley's new manager, Colonel Tom Parker, arranged for RCA Records to purchase the young singer's record contract from Sun Records for the sum of $35,000. Phillips reluctantly accepted RCA's offer. The Sun Records owner was sad to lose his biggest star, but with all the new acts he had recently signed, he was already too busy to worry about it.

With Tom Parker and RCA behind him, Presley quickly achieved the same level of success nationwide that he had enjoyed regionally with Sun. In little more than six months, he virtually conquered the *Billboard* singles charts, laying claim to the number-one country single ("I Forgot to Remember to Forget"), the number-one rhythm-and-blues single ("Heartbreak Hotel"), and the number-one pop single ("I Want You, I Need You, I Love You").

Inevitably, there was a backlash against Presley's sudden success, and the new type of music that he had helped to make popular. Religious leaders, parents and teachers organizations, politicians, and the mainstream music industry all found reasons to condemn both Elvis and rock and roll. "He can't sing a lick," wrote journalist Jack O'Brien in 1956, barely concealing the racism of his remarks, "[and] makes up for vocal short-comings with the weirdest and plainly planned suggestive animation short of an aborigine's mating dance."[5] The pressure from conservative groups became so intense that on many of his televised performances during the period, Presley was only shown from the waist up. Apparently, many older viewers were offended by the suggestive way the young singer wiggled his hips when he danced.

Though his comments were not intended specifically for Presley, Frank Sinatra echoed the opinions of many older performers toward Elvis and his music when he made the following remarks to the press in 1957. "Rock 'n' roll smells phony and false," complained the popular singer about the new music's sudden popularity. "It is sung, played, and written for the most part by cretinous goons and by means of its almost imbecilic reiteration, and sly, lewd, in plain fact, dirty lyrics . . . it manages to be the martial music of every sideburned delinquent on the face of the earth. . . . It is," concluded Sinatra with a flair, "the most brutal, ugly, desperate, vicious form of expression it has been my misfortune to hear."[6]

Presley took it all in stride, however. During the next year and a half, he and his music dominated both the nation's record sales and its imagination. In the midst of his hectic schedule of touring, movie roles, and television appearances, he released a remarkable string of hit singles that included "Hound Dog," "Don't Be Cruel," "Love Me Tender," "Jailhouse Rock," "All Shook Up," and "Teddy Bear." By the time he was drafted by the U.S. Army in 1958, Presley had already sold more than 16 million records for RCA and established himself as one of the dominant figures in the history of popular music. Presley continued to enjoy hit singles both during and after his tour of duty in the army, including two greatest-hits albums released while he was serving in Germany.

Though Presley left the United States in 1958 as a rock-and-roll phenomenon, he returned as a motion-picture star. Even before he left for Germany, he had already appeared in four successful films: 1956's *Love Me Tender*, 1957's *Loving You* and *Jailhouse*

THE HISTORY OF ROCK AND ROLL

Rock, and 1958's *King Creole*. On his return, he devoted himself almost exclusively to a string of commercially successful but less ambitious Hollywood musicals. The formula for his films was always the same: Elvis would play the romantic lead opposite one of the film studio's most popular young actresses, performing a new batch of songs both in the movie and on a simultaneously released sound-track recording.

For more than a decade, Presley's films remained popular at the box office, and though he stopped releasing hit singles after 1962, his soundtrack albums continued to go gold. The sound track to *Blue Hawaii* alone sold more than five million copies in its first year of release. But he had stopped touring and keeping up with the new forces that were shaping popular music, and the quality of his music suffered terribly. By the early 1960s, Presley was no longer a major force in rock and roll, although his early recordings with Sun and RCA would continue to inspire a new generation of rock-and-roll musicians.

In December 1968, Presley made a brief and successful attempt to reestablish himself as a rock-and-roll performer, appearing in his own one-hour, prime-time television special. For the centerpiece of the program, Presley joined guitarist Scotty Moore and drummer D. J. Fontana to perform several of his old hits for a small studio audience. Presley's vocals were a bit rough compared to the recordings of his youth, and the arrangements were surprisingly simple. Without a drum kit, Fontana simply tapped his sticks on the side of his chair. But everyone watching the program could tell that the singer was genuinely enjoying himself, and most critics considered Presley's performance to be his most inspired public appearance in more than a decade. By the fall of the following year, "Suspicious Minds," a soulful new song that Presley had introduced during the television special, had reached number one on the pop singles charts. It was Presley's first number-one single since 1962.

Rather than returning to the rock-and-roll circuit, however, Presley used his newfound respectability as a live performer to establish himself as a Las Vegas entertainer. During the 1970s, millions of fans traveled to Nevada to see him trudge through over-arranged, carefully choreographed versions of his classic hits from the 1950s. For a new generation of listeners, Presley would simply be known as the King, an overweight, middle-aged lounge singer with aviator sunglasses, dyed black hair, and a white, sequined jump suit.

At the time of Presley's death from a drug overdose in August 1977, popular music in the United States had once again become almost completely segregated for black and white listeners. In the days following Presley's death, rock critic Lester Bangs remembered the groundbreaking role that Presley had played in bringing black and white listeners together more than 20 years earlier. "I can guarantee you one thing," wrote Bangs at the end of his remarks, "we will never again agree on anything as we agreed on Elvis."[7]

2 "HAIL, HAIL, ROCK AND ROLL"

With Elvis Presley conquering the pop charts toward the end of 1955, talent scouts across the country began looking for new artists who could match the young Memphis singer's success. One of the things that made Elvis's recordings so important was the uniqueness of his sound. In the early 1950s, major labels made a regular practice of rerecording the minor hits released by small recording companies and turning them into smash hits of their own. Popular songs by young rock-and-roll artists like Fats Domino and Lloyd Price were frequently covered by mainstream performers like Pat Boone. Geared toward a white middle-class audience, the new, less daring versions often sold 10 times as many copies as the originals. It was not unusual during the 1950s for as many as three versions of the same song to appear on the singles charts at the same time. Such a situation made it almost impossible for the small rock-and-roll-oriented labels to achieve success. Increasingly, their goal became to find other artists, like Elvis, who were either so talented and unique—or so outrageous—that their styles could not be easily imitated by artists on the major labels.

It would be hard to imagine a rock-and-roll performer with a musical style that was more difficult to imitate than "Little Richard" Penniman. Little Richard was born in 1932 in Macon, Georgia, the same sleepy southern town that produced rhythm-and-blues standouts James Brown and Otis Redding. Richard grew up in a large African-American household where the smooth, soothing music of crooner Bing Crosby and jazz diva Ella Fitzgerald were more popular than the hard-driving beats of blues and rhythm and blues. But Richard soon discovered a different style of music in the energetic, emotionally charged services of the black Pentecostal church where his cousin Amos was a minister. Totally uninhibited as a child, Richard—with his pure tenor voice and his early gifts as a musician—soon made his own unique contribution to the church's inspired music.

"I used to play piano for the church," he would later explain to *Rolling Stone*'s David Dalton. "You know that spiritual, 'Give Me That Old Time Religion'? Most churches just say, 'Give me that old time religion,' but I did, 'Give me that old time, talkin' 'bout religion.' I put that little *thing* in it, you know. I always did have that *thing*."[8]

By the time he was a teenager, Richard had graduated from the choir loft in Macon to the bandstands of Atlanta, headlining for various swing and rhythm-and-blues bands in the capital city's dance halls and night clubs. Even in the larger ensembles with which he performed during this period, Richard always made sure that he was the center of attention. Both on and off the stage, he wore brightly colored suits, high-heeled shoes, a neatly trimmed pencil-thin mustache, and a huge, brushed-back pompadour haircut that sometimes rose several inches above his head. Robert "Bumps" Blackwell, who would later become Richard's manager, appreciated Richard's outrageous sense of style the first time they met. "He was so far out!" Blackwell later told an interviewer with a laugh. "His hair was processed a foot high over his head. His shirt was so loud it looked as though he had drunk raspberry juice, cherryade, malt, and greens and then thrown up all over himself. Man, he was a freak!"[9]

By 1950, Richard was already a versatile vocalist and musician with an outrageously entertaining stage act. Soon, he was attracting the attention of the record company scouts who combed Atlanta's clubs each night in search of new talent. In the early 1950s, he recorded a number of singles for RCA and Peacock Records with the Johnny Otis Orchestra and his own band, the Tempo Toppers. Unlike his live performances, however, Richard's early recordings were moody and restrained, attracting little interest from radio listeners or record buyers. He would have to wait a few more years before he found a way to capture the excitement of his stage act on record.

Bumps Blackwell came to know Little Richard in 1955. Blackwell was working as a talent scout for Specialty Records, trying to find "a new Ray Charles" for his boss Art Rupe. A blind piano player from Albany, Georgia, with a rich baritone singing voice, Charles favored a hard, explosive style of rhythm and blues that provided Atlantic Records with a number of successful records among black buyers during the early 1950s. In 1955, Charles's stark, emotionally charged single, "I Got a Woman," caught on with white audiences as well and reached the top of the singles charts. A remake of an old gospel standard, "I Got a Savior," the song combined the urgency of gospel music with the hard, driving beat of rhythm and blues. A seasoned veteran in the music business, Art Rupe felt certain that both black and white listeners were eager to buy more records that sounded like Charles's latest hit. With this in mind, he sent Blackwell in search of a new black performer who could compete with the Atlantic recording artist.

Although Richard's early singles were mediocre at best, Blackwell knew the moment he heard them that he had found his "new Ray Charles." "The voice was unmistakably star material," he would later recall. "I can't tell you how I knew, but I knew. I could tell by the tone of his voice and all those churchy tunes that he was a gospel singer who could sing the blues."[10]

At his first full recording session for Specialty Records, in New Orleans on September 13 and 14, 1955, Little Richard more than lived up to Blackwell's expectations. Richard and his band, the Tempo Toppers, performed a dozen tracks of riveting rock and roll that had far more energy and excitement than even the best of Charles's latest recordings. The recording sessions almost failed to happen, however, owing to—of all things—Little Richard's embarrassment over performing one of his songs.

The first song chosen for the session, "Tutti Frutti," was a bawdy, hard-rocking dance tune typical of the music that Richard and his band played each night in beer halls, burlesques, and gay bars throughout the south. Blackwell realized that the song's normal lyrics were too sexually suggestive to be played on the radio, however. At the last minute, he brought songwriter Dorothy La Bastrie into the studio to listen to the song and provide Richard with a new, more socially acceptable set of lyrics.

Richard had already been delighting the studio crew with his spirited performances during rehearsals. But he took one look at the tiny, attractive young lyricist and became suddenly shy and withdrawn, refusing to play the song as long as she remained in the studio. For most of the day, Richard stuck to his guns, performing several less offensive—and less exciting—numbers with his band. Finally, only 15 minutes before the session was scheduled to end, Blackwell presented Richard with a completely new set of lyrics for "Tutti Frutti" that La Bastrie had penned that afternoon in the studio, without the benefit of having heard him perform the tune. At first Richard still refused to sing, claiming that his throat was sore from a full day of recording. After reading through the song's new lyrics, however, he turned back toward the piano and charged right into the tune.

With Little Richard's hammered keyboard introduction and the song's unforgettable opening phrase, "Awop bop a loo mop a lop bam boom!," "Tutti Frutti" was soon blaring out of radio and phonograph speakers around the country. The song was louder,

Little Richard rollicks during a 1957 performance. The flamboyant singer produced some of the finest rock-and-roll songs of the late 1950s.

wilder, and more exciting than anything most listeners had ever heard before. As the single began to climb steadily up the rhythm-and-blues charts, Rupe and Blackwell felt confident that they had finally released a hit song that no mainstream artist from a major label could possibly imitate. They were wrong, however. Both Pat Boone and Elvis Presley immediately released their own covers of "Tutti Frutti," with Boone's version reaching number one on *Billboard*'s pop singles charts.

In spite of Boone's success with the song, Little Richard's original version of "Tutti Frutti" remained enormously popular, selling more than one million copies before it slipped off the rhythm-and-blues charts after 15 weeks. Both Blackwell and Little Richard, however, were determined that *no one* was going to duplicate the performer's next single, "Long Tall Sally." Richard's harsh, staccato vocals on the number represent what may be the finest, most exhilarating vocal performance of the era. The tune, with its B-side, "Slippin' and Slidin'," quickly sold more than half a million copies, climbing all the way into the top 20 of *Billboard*'s pop singles charts within a few weeks of its release. Remarkably, Pat Boone did release his own version of the song, a comically inept piece of fluff that quietly sold a million copies. By this time, however, no one, anywhere, could possibly mistake Boone's smooth crooning for the real, original version of the song—or fail to recognize that Little Richard Penniman was the one true wild man of rock and roll.

Little Richard's greatest period of success was in late 1956 and early 1957, during which he released an incredible string of hits that included "She's Got It," "Heeby-Jeebies," "Lucille," "Jenny, Jenny," and "The Girl Can't Help It." The latter single was the title cut for a popular "rock-and-roll movie" starring Jayne Mansfield and featuring live performances by Richard, Fats Domino, Gene Vincent, Eddie Cochran, and the Platters. Filmed in color, the movie was a huge success, and gave young people across the nation their first chance to see their rock-and-roll idols perform their hits in concert.

In spite of his success, Richard was rarely happy during this period, however. Even with his wild, unconventional behavior, he was always very serious about his roots in the black Pentecostal church. He was deeply troubled whenever a conservative columnist condemned his outrageous live performances or a radio station refused to play one of his songs because of its sexually suggestive lyrics. Richard was also guilt-ridden about his lifestyle as a rock-and-roll performer. He drank heavily, used illegal drugs, and sometimes had sexual relations with other men. From time to time, he threatened to quit rock and roll and return to the church of his youth. Given the level of his success—and the fact that he continued his wild behavior—few people took his threats very seriously. That changed, however, in October 1957, when Little Richard and his band were in Australia for a two-week tour.

Accompanying Richard on the tour were fellow rockers Eddie Cochran and Alys Leslie, billed as the female Elvis Presley. The group had already performed for three days in Melbourne before arriving in Sydney to play at the city's 40,000-seat outdoor arena. Earlier in the day, the Soviet Union had successfully launched Sputnik I, the first artificial satellite, into orbit around the earth. In the middle of the concert, Richard suddenly caught a glimpse of the rocket's brilliant path across the night sky. Unaware that he was watching a Soviet satellite, Richard thought the light was a sign from God.

"It looked as though the big ball of fire came directly over the stadium about two or three hundred feet above our heads," he later explained to his biographer Charles White. "It shook my mind. It really shook my mind. I got up from the piano and said, 'This is it. I am through. I am leaving show business to go back to God.' "[11]

To demonstrate that his decision was sincere and not simply a publicity stunt, Richard spontaneously pulled an $8,000 gold ring from his finger and hurled it into the dark waters of Sydney Harbor. A few days later, Richard and the band were back in New York, his impulsive decision somewhat shaken by the news of the Soviet space mission. Richard's faith was renewed the following week, however, when the plane on which the band was originally scheduled to return to the United States crashed into the Pacific Ocean. There were no survivors. Richard Penniman soon found himself enrolled at a Pentecostal bible college in Huntsville, Alabama, studying the New Testament and church history.

To no one's surprise, Little Richard's career as a ministerial student was a brief one. The school's administrators were understandably concerned by the former rock-and-roll performer's pink Cadillac, flashy clothing, and all-night partying. By 1959, Richard had returned to popular music, recording a number of rollicking gospel tracks on George Goldner's End and Goldisc labels. Eventually, Richard would leave gospel behind completely and begin playing rock and roll again with the same energy and flair he had first demonstrated during the mid-1950s. He would never again regain the enormous popularity that he had enjoyed during that period, but his powerful vocal style would leave its mark on a new generation of rock-and-roll performers, such as the Beatles' Paul McCartney, the Rolling Stones' Mick Jagger, and John Fogerty of Creedence Clearwater Revival. Richard's singles on Specialty Records rank among the most joyous and energetic rock-and-roll recordings ever made.

The only contemporary rock-and-roll artist who could match Little Richard's outrageous performing style was a young, blond-haired piano player from Ferriday, Louisiana, named Jerry Lee Lewis. The cousin of country singer Mickey Gilley and evangelist Jimmy Swaggart, Lewis originally wanted to be a piano-pounding Pentecostal minister like his older cousin Jimmy. After a short stint at the Southwestern Bible Institute in Waxahachie, Texas, however, Lewis was expelled from both the school and the denomination for his devil-inspired instrumental technique. Though it broke his heart to leave the church, Jerry Lee agreed with his teachers' assessment of his performances. No matter how hard he tried to restrain his playing to meet the needs of the pastor or the choir, however, the keys seemed to dance beneath his fingers all by themselves. He sometimes found himself hammering out rock-and-roll rhythms right in the middle of the worship service.

"Man, I got the devil in me," he once confessed to Sam Phillips in the middle of a recording session. "If I didn't, I'd be a Christian."[12]

After leaving the church, Lewis eventually made his way to Memphis, Tennessee, and Sun Records, where Phillips was already building an impressive lineup of rock-and-roll performers that included Carl Perkins, Johnny Cash, Roy Orbison, and Billy Lee Riley. Lewis played piano on a number of Perkins's and Riley's singles before getting a chance to record his own single toward the end of 1956. The slow two-step rhythms of "Crazy Arms" had proven ideal for country singer Ray Price, who had a hit with the song earlier in the year. It was a poor choice as a first single for Lewis, however, drawing too much attention to his limited vocal range while keeping him from displaying his extraordinary skills as a pianist.

Things improved the following year, however, when Phillips and Lewis decided to record the backwoods-revival-inspired "Whole Lot of Shakin' Goin' On." With its hard keyboard rhythms,

Jerry Lee Lewis gives a hair-raising performance in June 1958. Many radio stations banned Lewis's records from the air when he married his 13-year-old cousin in 1958.

its left-handed boogie-woogie bass line, and the muted sensuality of Jerry Lee's growling vocals, the song displayed the newcomer as a formidable force in rock-and-roll music. A few weeks after the record's release, Lewis drew even more attention to himself during a controversial televised performance on the popular "Steve Allen Show." Midway though his song, Lewis kicked his piano stool out from under him and began pounding the keys like a madman. Allen, the program's host, seemed to love it, showering Lewis with various stray objects from the studio. Reviewers were scandalized by Lewis' performance, teenage audiences across the nation were delighted, and Lewis had become an overnight sensation.

Lewis was soon nicknamed the Killer, because of his harsh, violent performance style and his equally outrageous behavior off the stage. He followed the success of "Whole Lot of Shakin' Goin' On" with a string of hit singles that included "Breathless," "Crazy," and "Great Balls of Fire." From the beginning of his career, however, Lewis seemed determined to destroy his newly achieved success. Like Little Richard, he was always alienating his friends and fellow performers with his constant bragging, and his drinking and partying frequently got him into trouble.

Things reached their lowest point in 1958 when Lewis, who had already been married twice before, decided to wed his 13-year-old third cousin, Myra Gale. Phillips and the record company managed to keep the matter out of the news for several months. With typical arrogance, Jerry Lee decided to break the news himself to— of all people—the notoriously conservative British press. Arriving at London's Heathrow Airport for his first tour of England, Lewis appeared before a team of English reporters with his new bride at his side. When the journalists asked about the young girl's identity, the performer acknowledged what most people in the crowd already suspected.

"She's my wife, Myra," he stated matter-of-factly.

When the reporters followed up with questions about Myra's age, Lewis lied and said that she was 15—an age that he assured the startled reporters was nowhere near too young for marriage back in his home state of Louisiana.

"Age doesn't matter back home," he lied again. "You can marry at ten, if you can find a bride."[13]

Lewis's manager, Oscar Davis, had done everything he could to discourage the recording artist from breaking the news so bluntly to the press. Jerry Lee could not be convinced, however. "Look," he told Davis, "people want me, and they're gonna take me, no matter what."[14]

Lewis, of course, was wrong about the tolerance of the record-buying public, both in England and the United States. In England, the story immediately became a public scandal. Negative coverage in the British tabloids resulted in poor attendance at many of the shows on the tour. Upset by the controversy, Lewis did little to improve his image among the faithful teenage fans who did buy tickets to his shows. Throughout the tour, he gave a series of uncharacteristically lackluster performances. At one show, he played only 10 minutes before getting up from his piano and walking silently off the stage.

Back in the United States, things were not quite as bad as they had been in England. A number of Lewis's friends and admirers in the media and entertainment industry continued to promote his music. The performer also managed to suppress his quick temper long enough to give a few thoughtful, well-rehearsed interviews with the American press. The release of Lewis's next single, however, the title cut from the movie *High School Confidential*, was simply too much for most fans to take. The song not only reminded the public of Lewis's unconventional marriage to a teenage girl; to many people, it seemed as if the singer, by releasing the song, was mocking the public's concern. Soon, popular music programs like Dick Clark's *American Bandstand* were refusing to allow Lewis to perform, and sales for the singer's recordings slowly began to decline. It was a fall in popularity from which Lewis would never fully recover.

SCREAMIN' JAY HAWKINS

For more than 40 years, rhythm-and-blues shouter Screamin' Jay Hawkins has been thrilling—and occasionally frightening—fans with his powerful baritone voice and weird antics onstage. Even in the mid-1950s, when Little Richard and Jerry Lee Lewis were at the height of their outlandish showmanship, Hawkins was unrivaled for his creativity and audacity in performance. To start each show, he would slowly emerge from a coffin that had been placed at center stage, with his shoulders draped in a Dracula-style cape and a red-eyed human skull mounted on the end of his cane. But Hawkins never really needed the props to get his audience's attention. He used his huge, thundering voice to give songs like "I Put a Spell on You" and "Alligator Wine" their dark, eerie effects. Sadly, the same bizarre theatrics that earned Hawkins acclaim in concert kept most critics and record buyers from taking his recorded music very seriously. After a couple of minor hits in the late 1950s, he was reduced primarily to a novelty act, playing small clubs and an occasional rock-and-roll revival. In the mid-1980s, Hawkins enjoyed a brief comeback following the success of the independent feature film *Mystery Train*, an offbeat comedy by director Jim Jarmusch. The film featured "I Put a Spell on You" in its sound track.

While Little Richard and the Killer were thrilling audiences with their flamboyant piano techniques, another young composer was about to transform the electric guitar into rock and roll's main instrument. St. Louis native Chuck Berry was still working at his day job as a hair stylist when the great blues singer, Muddy Waters, caught his act at a small blues club in Chicago in 1955. To Waters's ears, Berry's songs were nothing special; most of them were tired country ballads already covered better by other artists. And there was little to get excited about in Berry's thin, monotone vocal delivery. But Waters was immediately impressed by the way Berry played his guitar. Throughout his concerts, Berry filled his country ballads with the full guitar chordings and hammered leads he had learned by listening to the innovative 1940s Texas blues guitarist T-Bone Walker. Berry's improbable blend of country phrasings, rhythm-and-blues beats, and powerful blues guitar was something new and exciting.

The most popular and respected musician on the Chicago blues scene, Waters took pride in discovering new artists and new styles of music. He immediately introduced Berry to his bosses at Chess Records. During the 1950s, Leonard and Cliff Chess made a name for themselves recording and promoting blues musicians like Waters and Chester "Howlin' Wolf" Burnett. But they were always interested in discovering new talent, especially if they thought it would appeal to the younger generation of record buyers. Earlier in the year, they had signed another hot young guitarist, Ellas "Bo Diddley" McDaniels, whose spirited, bass-heavy single, "Hey, Bo Diddley" / "I'm a Man," had recently peaked near the top of the rhythm-and-blues charts. Along with Waters, the Chess brothers felt confident that Berry's new sound would appeal to the same young audience that was currently dancing to Diddley's latest tunes.

Berry's first recording for Chess Records was "Maybellene," a loud, jangling remake of Lloyd "Cowboy" Copas's country hit, "Ida Red." Within four weeks of its release, "Maybellene" had reached the top of the rhythm-and-blues charts. The song was so popular, in fact, that it quickly crossed over to the *Billboard* pop singles charts, where it easily outlasted and outsold remakes by such popular mainstream acts as the Ralph Marterie Orchestra and the Johnny Long Orchestra. The Chess brothers realized they had found a sound that the major labels would not be easily able to copy, and they put their full support behind their new star.

Berry's stage act was every bit as unusual as his sound on record. For one thing, the guitarist was almost comically attentive to his appearance. His jet black hair was slicked back and immaculately groomed, his shirts were ruffled, and his tuxedo coats were brightly colored and often covered with sequins. When the time came to play his guitar leads, he turned to the side and stood with his profile facing the audience, thrusting his guitar out from his hip like a gun he was firing toward someone offstage.

The oddest and most popular part of Berry's act was his famous duck walk. Sometimes in the middle of his guitar solos, he would raise one leg from the floor and lurch across the stage on the other leg in time with the throbbing rhythm of the music. Crowds everywhere would go wild the second he started his routine, and performers across the nation tried in vain to copy his unique style.

According to Berry, the "duck walk" originated by accident during his first performance at the Paramount Theater in New York in 1956. For the occasion, Berry had bought a brand new wardrobe for his band that included yellow jackets, pink trousers, and bright blue shoes. The suits became badly wrinkled during the trip to New York, however, and Berry, who was always a perfectionist about his appearance, was embarrassed to take the stage. "The suits," he recalled to an interviewer in 1969, "they were

The dapper Chuck Berry struts his stuff for this early publicity shot.

rayon, but looked like seersucker by the time we got there. So I actually did the duck walk to hide the wrinkles in the suit. I got an ovation. So I figured I pleased the crowd, so I did it again, and again, and I'll probably do it again tonight."[15]

During the next two years, Berry released one hit record after another for Chess Records. His follow-up single to "Maybellene," "Roll Over, Beethoven," was an inspiring, self-congratulatory anthem to the new style of music that artists like Berry, Little Richard, Elvis Presley, and Jerry Lee Lewis were introducing to the public. The song was an open challenge to music's old guard—not just classical composers like Beethoven and Tchaikovsky but the heroes of traditional forms of music like country, jazz, and the blues. With his outrageously self-confident lyrics and furious guitar playing throughout the song, Berry made a strong case that he had come to take their place.

On "School Day (Ring, Ring Goes the Bell)," Berry dared to say what every healthy teenager in America already knew: that high school was boring and oppressive, and the day's happiest moment was the pealing of the three o'clock bell. "Hail, hail, rock and roll!," began the song's final chorus. Berry's song was a joyous celebration of the new lifestyle—and the new form of music—that had come to take high school's place. Berry was in his late twenties when "School Day" was released in the spring of 1957, but more than any other composer of his time, he had found a voice for the desires and emotions of teenage listeners.

Berry's finest moment came the following year, however, with the release of "Johnny B. Goode." The song told the story of a young guitarist who dreamed of becoming a rock-and-roll star. Wherever the song was played, its furiously repeated chorus, "Go, Johnny, go, go, go," became an irresistible chant for every youngster who was frustrated with his or her life and longed for something better. "Johnny B. Goode" also provided Berry with one of his signature guitar performances, opening with a lightning-fast, four-measure solo that dropped suddenly into the hard, bumpy rhythm that pushed the words along. Berry's frantic performance on "Johnny B. Goode" would inspire countless future rock-and-roll guitarists, including Jimi Hendrix, the Rolling Stones' Keith Richard, and, sadly, Berry himself. In later years, having apparently run out of new ideas, Berry frequently recycled his old themes and guitar licks whenever he needed a new song.

Like the turbulent careers of Little Richard and Jerry Lee Lewis, Berry's reign at the top of the emerging rock-and-roll empire ended suddenly. Early in 1960, the singer was arrested on the charge of illegally carrying a 14-year-old girl across a state line. It was later determined that the girl had made up the charges because she was angry at Berry, who had recently fired her from her job as a hat-check girl at his Club Bandstand in St. Louis. In the meantime, however, the damage had been done. Berry, who had already served a brief prison term during the 1940s, was viewed by the public as an accused child molester. His latest two-sided single, "Back in the U.S.A." / "Memphis," began to drop steadily from the charts, and Berry's public appearances became less and less frequent. Although a later generation would proclaim him as one of the true pioneers of rock and roll, he would never again regain the enormous popularity or creativity that he had enjoyed during the late 1950s.

3

THE DAY THE MUSIC DIED

The excitement and raw energy of early rock and roll resulted from the loud, uneasy mixture of several different musical traditions. If you listened closely enough to the early songs of Elvis Presley, Chuck Berry, Little Richard, or Jerry Lee Lewis, you could hear elements of blues, gospel, country and western, boogie-woogie, and rhythm and blues. The best rock-and-roll musicians found a way to combine these different styles to create music that sounded like much more than the sum of its parts. However listeners may have felt about their first exposure to "Hound Dog," "Johnny B. Goode," "Great Balls of Fire" and "Long, Tall Sally"—and most older listeners hated what they heard—everyone agreed that this was definitely a type of music that they had never heard before.

This, in large part, accounts for the extraordinary success of Elvis Presley. In Elvis, Sam Phillips had not simply found, as some listeners claimed, a white man who could sing like a black man. Instead, Phillips had discovered something much more special: a young white musician who had somehow tapped into the confusion and excitement that was already transforming black music around the nation. Presley may have sold more records than Little

Richard primarily because of the color of his skin, but rock and roll was neither black music nor white music. It was, from the beginning, an exciting mix of the two. And that, more than anything else, accounts for rock and roll's enormous appeal to the millions of young listeners who were struggling to define themselves and their world during the mid-1950s.

Ironically, it was the incredible success of Presley and other mainstream rock-and-roll musicians that led to the music's gradual decline as the decade drew to a close. As commercial radio and record companies became more daring in the mid-1950s, young musicians spent more of their time listening to established stars and less time checking out the less popular musicians and styles of music that had inspired artists like Presley and Little Richard in the first place. This was particularly true for the young country-inspired rockabilly musicians who looked to Presley for their inspiration.

"Most rockabilly musicians," rock critic Greil Marcus would observe almost 20 years later, "weren't even imitating blacks, let alone listening to the inner voice Sam Phillips wanted to hear; they were imitating Elvis."[16]

In his earliest—and best—recordings, Presley sounded like something completely new: not quite country, not quite western swing, and not quite rhythm and blues. Sadly, most of the rockabilly singers who grew up on a steady diet of Presley's music sounded like little more than second-rate Elvises.

There were exceptions, of course. Throughout the remainder of the decade, hard rockabilly performers like Eddie Cochran and Gene Vincent continued to make fierce, uncompromising music. In 1957, Don and Phil Everly, a country duet from Kentucky, began mixing the high, smooth harmonies of bluegrass with an aggressive rock-and-roll beat. Strumming away at their acoustic guitars, the

Everly Brothers brought both energy and sweetness to a run of popular singles that included the classics "Bye Bye Love" and "Wake Up, Little Susie."

The most notable exception to rock and roll's artistic decline was the brilliant, innovative music of Charles Hardin "Buddy" Holly. A native of Lubbock, Texas, Holly and his partner Bob Montgomery were trying to make their mark as a country swing duo when they first heard Presley play in a Lubbock nightclub during the fall of 1955. For some time, the two young men had been trying without success to bring the excitement of rhythm and blues into their country performances. To Holly's keen ear, Presley had somehow found the secret that had been eluding the Lubbock combo. Holly was so impressed, in fact, that he actually got up the nerve to approach Elvis after the concert to express his enthusiasm. Exhausted by the show, Presley had collapsed in a corner of the club with a bottle of soda, but he talked politely with the energetic young musician for several minutes. Before Holly walked nervously away, Presley encouraged him to continue his career. "You know," Holly later repeated to his manager, Hipockets Duncan, "he's a real nice, friendly fellow."[17]

Hearing and meeting Presley inspired Holly and Montgomery to give their live performances a harder rhythm-and-blues edge. Their new, rowdier style bewildered the older country music purists who owned the local nightclubs and radio stations. Lubbock's younger music listeners loved the duo's new sound, however, and Holly and Montgomery soon developed a large, enthusiastic group of teenage fans who shouted requests for the band's louder rockabilly numbers wherever the duo played. Finally, in October 1955, the band's growing popularity attracted the attention of Decca Records, who approached Holly with a record deal. There was one major problem, however. The label was only interested in Buddy and the new numbers that he had recently written for the band. "You can bring [Bob Montgomery] along if you want," Decca representative Jim Denny told him at the time, "but he can't sing on the records. We want one singer, not two."[18] With Montgomery's encouragement and support, Holly reluctantly accepted Decca's offer. After years of developing his sound along with his partner Montgomery, he was suddenly facing his future as a solo act.

Holly's first single for Decca, "Love Me," enjoyed modest success on the country charts. But the label soon lost confidence in the young rockabilly singer. By the time his second single, "Modern Don Juan," was released toward the end of 1956, Holly and Decca were ready to call it quits. Determined to get his music to the public on his own terms, Buddy made arrangements to record some of his new tunes for Norman Petty, a song publisher who owned and operated his own recording studio in Clovis, New Mexico. Early in 1957, Buddy and his new band, the Crickets, drove to Petty's studio and recorded two songs, "I'm Looking for Someone to Love" and "That'll Be the Day." Buddy had already recorded "That'll Be the Day" for Decca the previous year, but the new version was arranged and recorded strictly according to his own standards.

Jointly released by Petty's Nor Va Jay label and Peer-Southern Records, "That'll Be the Day" soon began to climb the charts. By August, the single had peaked at number two on *Billboard*'s rhythm-and-blues charts, and Petty was eager to record more singles with Holly and his band.

Throughout the following year, Buddy Holly and the Crickets released one classic rock-and-roll single after another, including "Oh, Boy!," "Not Fade Away," "Every Day," "It's So Easy to Fall in Love," and the smash hit, "Peggy Sue." On the latter song, Buddy introduced the public to the grunting, hiccuping vocal technique that would become his trademark. At the end of certain phrases, he would quickly inhale in the middle of the final note. This produced the gasping vocal urgency that was commonly used by Pentecostal preachers and hard rhythm-and-blues singers like James Brown. Holly was the first white rock-and-roll performer to use the technique on a popular recording, however, and young listeners loved it. Every time the words, "Peggy Sue-uh, Peggy Sue-uh," rang out of a radio speaker or throughout a concert hall, teenagers across the nation began to scream and clap their hands like Pentecostal worshipers at a revival meeting.

In March 1958, Buddy and the Crickets made a highly publicized tour of England, where they discovered that British teenagers liked their bouncy rockabilly music as much as young people in the United States. Holly wanted to be more than just a teenage idol, however, and he soon began to experiment with a fuller, gentler sound that would appeal to a broader audience. Toward the end of 1958, he released a single of Canadian pop singer Paul Anka's "It Doesn't Matter Anymore" that included a full string arrangement. Norman Petty and the Crickets did not share Buddy's ambition to become mainstream performers, however, and they withdrew their support from his newest projects. As 1958 drew to a close, Holly found himself with neither a manager nor a full-time band.

When Holly was invited to join the "Winter Dance Party" in January 1959, he jumped at the chance—even without a band. A two-week tour of the northern Midwest, the "Dance Party" featured such popular rock-and-roll acts as Dion and the Belmonts, Frankie Sardo, J. P. "the Big Bopper" Richardson, and Latino sensation, Ritchie Valens. Valens's fast, spirited version of the Mexican folk song "La Bamba" had just become an enormous hit both in the United States and abroad. Buddy quickly put together a backup band for the tour that included guitarist Tommy Allsup, Charlie Bunch on drums, and bass player Waylon Jennings, a local disc jockey who would later become a country music star.

It was a particularly brutal winter throughout the Midwest, and the tour members were overwhelmed with weather-related problems from the start. The buses were poorly heated and continually broke down, and many of the roads along their route were closed because of ice and snow. One night, Charlie Bunch developed frostbite in his feet while waiting outside for a bus to be repaired and had to leave the tour.

After several days of discomfort and inconvenience, Holly decided that he had endured enough lengthy delays and cold nights on the tour bus. On February 1, following a two-show stop in Wisconsin and yet another freezing night on the bus, he made arrangements with a local airplane service to fly him and his remaining band members from Mason City, Minnesota, to the tour's next stop in Fargo, North Dakota. When headliners J. P. Richardson and Ritchie Valens heard about Holly's plans, they persuaded Jennings and Allsup to give up their seats on the plane and endure the cold, uncomfortable bus for one more night. Allsup was reluctant to return to the bus, and he only relinquished his seat to Valens when he lost it in a coin toss.

The plane's pilot, Roger Peterson, was a young aviator with very little experience flying in stormy winter weather. In addition, the traffic controllers at the Mason City airport failed to inform Peterson that the weather along his route that night would be so stormy and his visibility so poor that he would have to navigate the tiny four-seat plane completely by the use of the instruments in the cockpit.

As the group left the ground, the plane service's owner, Jerry Dwyer, could see from the control room that Peterson was having trouble keeping the aircraft steady. Unable to contact Peterson by radio, he spent a frantic, sleepless night contacting every airport in the area to see if the plane had been forced to make an emergency landing. As dawn approached, neither Fargo nor any of the neighboring airports had seen or heard from the plane. Desperate, Dwyer jumped into another airplane and began to search for his pilot and the missing passengers.

"I just couldn't sit there," he later recalled, "and decided I would go fly and try to follow the same course that I thought Roger would have taken."[19]

Eight miles northwest of the Mason City airport, Dwyer spotted the crumpled remains of the airplane scattered across a small cornfield. The plane had apparently landed on its side, tearing off one of its wings, before skidding and bouncing into a wooden fence about 500 feet away. The coroner would later determine that all of the men had been killed instantly by the force of the crash.

The sudden death of Buddy Holly had a devastating impact on rock-and-roll music and the millions of young people who enjoyed it. With Elvis in the military, Little Richard in a Pentecostal seminary, and Jerry Lee Lewis's career in shambles, Holly had become for many people the last real hope for rock and roll. As the original hard-rocking musicians had disappeared from the scene, record companies and promoters had begun to replace them with milder, less-innovative performers. During the past few years, the outrageous lifestyles and impulsive decisions of entertainers like Little Richard and Jerry Lee Lewis had cost record companies a lot of money and embarrassment. Many record company executives were determined to find

Buddy Holly's career was cut short by a fatal plane crash in January 1959.

46

young performers who would appeal to teenage fans while not offending their parents.

With this in mind, record labels during the late 1950s increasingly began to sign new artists more for their good manners and good looks than for their musical ability. After Holly's death, names like Bobby Rydell, Bobby Vee, Jimmy Clanton, Frankie Avalon, and Fabian began to replace hard rockers like Eddie Cochran, Chuck Berry and Gene Vincent on the airwaves and the record charts. For the most part, these new teen idols could barely sing at all. Those, like Avalon and Vee, who could carry a tune for the length of a standard three-minute rock song had high, nasally tenor voices that were more suited for sweet, catchy pop tunes than hard, spirited rock and roll.

All the new stars were strikingly handsome, and they always looked good on record sleeves and on their frequent live appearances on the new wave of rock-oriented television programs like Dick Clark's *American Bandstand*. Clark was a Philadelphia disc jockey with a strong commitment to making rock-and-roll music more accessible and acceptable to mainstream America. Regular appearances on Clark's program played an important role in advancing the careers of Fabian and Frankie Avalon. Both young singers were high school students in Philadelphia, where the television program was taped each week.

Philadelphia's Chancellor Records, the label that launched the careers of both Fabian and Avalon, took great care both to select and to groom performers who would appeal to young record buyers. "We now run a school where we indoctrinate artists into show business," the label's owner Bob Marcucci later explained to a reporter. "We may sign them and spend three months schooling them before they cut their first record. We teach them how to walk, how to talk, and how to act on stage."[20] It would be hard to imagine Little Richard, Jerry Lee Lewis, or even a young Elvis Presley surviving for very long in such a rock-and-roll charm school.

Regarding his youngest star, Fabian, Marcucci openly confessed in the same interview: "It's true that he couldn't sing. He knew it and I knew it."[21] In fact, everyone who heard Fabian's early releases, such as "I'm in Love" and "I'm a Tiger," knew that the handsome, athletically built teenager simply could not carry a tune. No one seemed to care how he sounded, however; Fabian's natural good looks were more than enough to ensure his success. Along with Avalon, Vee, and Rydell, he released one hit after another during the late 1950s and early 1960s.

Of all the new teen idols to surface during the late 1950s, by far the most talented was Ricky Nelson. The son of successful band leader, Ozzie Nelson, Ricky and his older brother Dave had been regular cast members on their parents' popular television program, *The Adventures of Ozzie and Harriet*, for several years before the younger Nelson boy bought his first guitar. Eager to give his talented young son a break in the music business, Ozzie Nelson arranged a recording deal with Imperial Records, for whom 16-year-old Ricky released his first single, a soft, bouncy version of Fats Domino's "I'm Walkin'." The song quickly became a hit, and Ricky began to perform regularly before a national audience during the final segment of his parents' weekly television program. With a crowd of teenage girls screaming their approval in the background, the neatly dressed, rosy-cheeked youngster would lip-synch the words to his latest release.

Like Avalon, Fabian, and Rydell, Nelson was carefully groomed by the record company to ensure his success. Unlike his fellow teen idols, however, Nelson had a real, enduring commitment to the hard, jangling style of rock and roll perfected by Presley and Holly—a fact that was consistently reflected in his own

Ricky Nelson practices a song on the set of his parents' TV show.

recordings. Nelson may not have had anything new to offer rock-and-roll listeners, but he had a clear, confident baritone voice and an impeccable ear for rock-and-roll melodies. Along with "I'm Walkin'," Nelson's "It's Late" and "Hello, Mary Lou" were among the best releases of the era.

The end of the decade saw the emergence of two of popular music's most innovative and influential producers: Berry Gordy, Jr., and Phil Spector. Out of his Motown Records headquarters in Detroit, Berry produced early hit records by Smokey Robinson and

Mary Wells during 1960. Over the next 25 years, "Mr. Hitsville," as he was sometimes called, would introduce listeners to such popular rhythm-and-blues mainstays as Marvin Gaye, the Temptations, the Four Tops, Diana Ross and the Supremes, and the Jackson Five.

Pop composer Phil Spector began perfecting his "wall of sound" production style in the late 1950s. Using thundering bass drums, sparkling keyboards, and layers and layers of vocals, Spector brought his distinctive touch to the recordings of Ben E. King, the Crystals, the Chiffons, the Shirelles, and the Righteous Brothers. The latter group's 1965 hit, "You've Lost That Lovin' Feelin'," was one of the most powerful and dramatic releases in 1960s pop music.

In the first years of the 1960s, the most popular American rock-and-roll bands included the Seattle instrumental band, the Ventures, the Beach Boys, and the Four Seasons. On hits like "The Real McCoy" and "Walk, Don't Run," the Ventures introduced a style of frantic guitar-driven instrumental music that would be copied by numerous bands during the early part of the decade. The southern California vocal group, the Beach Boys, combined loose, twangy guitars and barbershop-style vocal harmonies to create "surf music," one of the most popular trends of the era. On bouncy, good-natured tunes like "Sherry," "Walk Like a Man," and "Big Girls Don't Cry," the Four Seasons used swirling harmonies to support lead singer Frankie Valli's squealing falsetto.

4
THE BRITISH INVASION

While the Four Seasons, surf music, and rhythm and blues were replacing rock and roll at the top of the U.S. charts during the early 1960s, a new wave of young musicians on the other side of the Atlantic Ocean were just beginning to discover 1950s-style rock and roll for themselves. In British cities like London, Manchester, and Liverpool, new rock-and-roll bands introduced their fans to their own versions of songs by Elvis Presley, Little Richard, Chuck Berry, Carl Perkins, Buddy Holly, and the Everly Brothers. Many young British bands were also discovering the harder, harsher rhythms of the blues. A few young English rock-and-roll bands began to include songs by such American blues masters as Muddy Waters, Howlin' Wolf, and Sonny Boy Williamson in their live repertoire.

When their future manager, Brian Epstein, first heard the Liverpool band the Beatles, in 1961, the group's performances were made up almost entirely of American rock-and-roll standards. Epstein could tell right away, however, that there was something special about the quartet. With its appealing lead singers, Paul McCartney, who also played bass, and John Lennon on guitar, the band combined the hard urgency of rock and roll with the light, melodic cheerfulness of pop groups like the Four Seasons. McCartney borrowed his falsetto howl from his idol, Little Richard, and Lennon had a bit of Chuck Berry's sneer in his voice on the band's hardest-rocking numbers. But the band's high, sweeping harmonies and light, jangling rhythms were all their own.

After several lengthy tours of Hamburg, Germany, the Beatles had developed into a tight, imaginative performance ensemble who lent their own distinctive sound to whatever type of music they played. To the boys in the band, the Beatles' unique sound was always nothing more than simple, straightforward rock and roll.

"The critics and the people who write about [the Beatles'] music have to call it something," explained guitarist George Harrison in 1963. "They didn't want to say it was rock 'n' roll because rock was supposed to have gone out about five years ago. They decided it wasn't really rhythm and blues, so they called it the Liverpool sound, which is stupid, really. As far as we're concerned, it's the same as the rock from five years ago."[22]

By the time they signed with Capitol Records toward the end of 1962, the Beatles had replaced their original drummer, Pete Best, with newcomer Richard Starkey, known to the group's fans as Ringo Starr. Lennon and McCartney had begun to add their own tunes to the band's song list. A few of their original songs—"Please, Please Me," "From Me to You" and "She Loves You"—had already been released as singles by small American labels like Veejay and Swan. It was only with Capitol's release of "I Want to Hold Your Hand," however, that the band really began to gain momentum. Released in the United States on January 13, 1963, the song took only two weeks to reach number one on the *Billboard* pop singles charts. By the time the band made its first live television appearance on the popular *Ed Sullivan Show* in February, "Beatlemania" had already taken the nation by storm. More than 73 million Americans watched the band's U.S debut, and the group's first album, *Meet the Beatles*, was already at the top of the album charts.

In what was known in the press as the "British Invasion," the Beatles' remarkable popularity was followed by successful U.S. releases and tours by a number of other new English rock-and-roll groups, including Gerry and the Pacemakers, the Dave Clark Five, and Freddie and the Dreamers. None of these bands, however, would come close to matching the Liverpool quartet's ability to generate hit records or their longevity on the charts. Almost seven years would pass before anyone would begin to challenge the Beatles' dominance of both the British and American music markets.

In 1965, the Beatles transplanted their newfound success to motion pictures, with the release of Richard Lester's *A Hard Day's Night*. In contrast to Elvis Presley, whose later films had diminished his standing in the rock and roll world, the Beatles' film debut was a complete success. The film's sound track, along with the sound track to another 1965 film, *Help*, would join the band's other albums in reaching the top of the charts.

The Beatles' finest achievement in 1965, however, was the release of *Rubber Soul*, their first full album of all original material. "We got completely involved in ourselves then," John Lennon would later explain of the Beatles' decision to base their reputation strictly on their own material. "Something just happened. We controlled it a bit, whatever it was we were putting over. We just decided to control it."[23]

Rubber Soul was an amazing achievement for a band that had begun its career covering other artists' tunes. With songs like "Norwegian Wood," "Nowhere Man," "Michelle," and "In My Life," it was the most impressive collection of original composi-

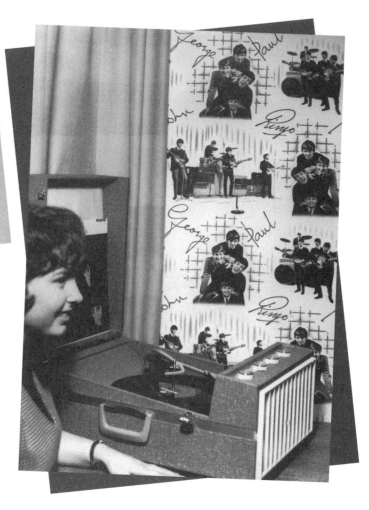

A young fan proudly shows off her Beatles wallpaper. John, Paul, George, and Ringo became the four most-famous people in the world simply by playing rock and roll.

tions that had ever been released by a rock-and-roll band or performer. The record immediately established Lennon and McCartney as the preeminent popular songwriting team of their generation. From *Rubber Soul* on, the Beatles' recordings set the standard not only for commercial success but for innovation and excellence in rock-and-roll music. *Rubber Soul* and the albums that followed it would inspire the best work of rock-and-roll artists as diverse as Bob Dylan, Frank Zappa, Brian Wilson, and the Rolling Stones.

The following year, John Lennon made an offhand remark at a press conference that threatened the Beatles' enormous popularity. Lennon, who was always the most outspoken and opinionated of the foursome, made the following statement when he was asked about his views on Christianity and the negative comments that some Christians had made about the Beatles' music.

"Christianity will go," he told the reporters matter-of-factly. "It will vanish and shrink. I needn't argue about that; I'm right and I will be proved right. We're more popular than Jesus now; I don't know which will go first, rock 'n' roll or Christianity. Jesus was all right, but his disciples were thick and ordinary. It's them twisting it that ruins it for me."[24]

Since the mid-1950s, conservative ministers and religious groups had used both the pulpit and the press to condemn rock and roll and the musicians who made it. Over the years, artists like Elvis Presley, Chuck Berry, and Jerry Lee Lewis had either ignored the criticism or, in the case of Little Richard, actually abandoned rock and roll for the church. In his comments to the press, Lennon was the first major rock-and-roll performer to stand up to the people who condemned him and his music. Unfortunately, in speaking out the way he did, he also offended many other religious people who enjoyed and supported the Beatles' music.

Lennon's controversial remarks to the press provoked an angry response from churches and religious groups throughout the United States, particularly in the South. During the next few weeks, thousands of teenage fans burned their Beatles records at highly publicized events around the country. But the controversy soon passed, and the band's popularity continued to grow.

In July 1967, the Beatles' highly anticipated album, *Sgt. Pepper's Lonely Hearts Club Band*, began to appear in record stores. For months, fans, critics, and other musicians had been eagerly awaiting the release of what was rumored to be the first rock-and-roll "concept album," a recording with lyrics and music united around a single theme. In fact, *Sgt. Pepper* turned out to be anything but a concept album. From the brass band fanfare of the opening title cut to the sad resignation of "A Day in the Life," the recording was an odd assortment of stories and musical styles that only the most imaginative young minds could hold together with a single concept or idea. No one seemed to notice that the album failed to live up to its promise, however. With producer George Martin's $100,000 production, Lennon and McCartney's consistently strong songs, and the innovative mix of traditional and avant-garde musical styles, *Sgt. Pepper* was the most influential and frequently discussed rock-and-roll album of the decade.

After the success of *Sgt. Pepper*, the Beatles gradually began to lose the edge to their music, if not the loyalty of their fans. For one thing, the band stopped playing together live, devoting their efforts exclusively to the studio. This decision inevitably caused the band members to lose touch with many of their fans. At a time when loud, aggressive live performances were becoming the main attraction of rock and roll, the Beatles continued to make sweet, melodic, intricately produced pop music.

The biggest blow, however, came in 1968 with the sudden, unexpected death of the band's longtime manager and friend, Brian Epstein. More than anyone else, Epstein had been responsible for holding the band's four talented and strong-willed members together as a single creative unit. With Epstein now out of the picture, the Beatles began to lose their focus. Each individual member began to take charge of the musical projects or business ventures that interested him the most.

The Beatles would have several more successful projects in the last years of the decade, including the made-for-television movie, *Magical Mystery Tour*, and the animated feature film, *Yellow Submarine*. But even the band's best releases, including *The White Album* and *Abbey Road*, were less Beatles recordings than collections of songs by the band's individual members. Introduced on the *Ed Sullivan Show* in 1969, the McCartney tune "Hey, Jude" would become the Beatles' biggest hit ever and one of the most successful singles in the history of popular music. At just over seven minutes, it was also one of the longest. Featuring some inspired screaming by McCartney on the final chorus, the song entered the charts at the number-ten position, remaining in the top 40 for an incredible 17 weeks.

For those who could listen between the lines, however, "Hey, Jude" revealed that the Beatles were in serious trouble. Many listeners felt that McCartney's accusing lyrics throughout the song were directed at band mate John Lennon. Lately, Lennon had been spending more and more of his time with his new wife, avant-garde artist Yoko Ono, and less and less time with the band. For his part, Lennon publicly accused McCartney of trying to take over the band and to use the other band members as a support group for his own musical projects. There were also rumors that George Harrison had become dissatisfied with the two compositions that he had been allowed per album and was eager to pursue a solo career.

"Spring is here and Leeds play Chelsea tomorrow," read the band's final 1970 press release, referring to a forthcoming rugby match, "and Ringo and John and George and Paul are alive and well and full of hope. The world is still spinning and so are we and so are you. When the spinning stops, that'll be the time to worry, not before. Until then, the Beatles are alive and well and the beat goes on, the beat goes on."[25]

By the end of the year, Lennon, McCartney, and Harrison had all released solo albums, and the Beatles were no more.

In addition to the Beatles' brilliant pop recordings, there was also a darker, more aggressive side to the British invasion of the mid-1960s. During the period, bands like the Animals, the Kinks, the Who, and the Rolling Stones introduced U.S. fans to their own hard, blues-inspired version of rock and roll.

The first British band to challenge the Beatles' cheerful style of rock and roll was the Animals. Headed by organist Alan Price and lead singer Eric Burdon, the band loaded its early song list with harsh, brooding versions of American blues and rhythm-and-blues standards. The band's biggest hit was 1964's "House of the Rising Sun," featuring a wild, growling lead vocal by Burdon.

The following year, the London band, the Kinks, became stars with throbbing, straightforward rock and roll on tunes like "You Really Got Me," "All Day and All of the Night," and "Tired of Waiting for You." However, the band's lead singer and songwriter, Ray Davies, was too musically sophisticated and ambitious to base his reputation on such simple, basic rock-and-roll arrangements. Beginning with 1965's "A Well Respected Man," the Kinks' song lyrics became more complex and demanding, and their sound was increasingly influenced by traditional British music. For the most part, American listeners simply were not interested in Davies' witty, ironic, dance-hall-style compositions. Though the band would release some of the more interesting rock-and-rock albums of the 1960s and 1970s—including *Face to Face*, *Muswell Hillbillies*, and *The Kink Kronikles*—they would never repeat the commercial success of their first few singles.

Led by guitarist Pete Townshend and vocalist Roger Daltrey, London's the Who started out as a cover band in the early 1960s, mixing Beatles songs and blues standards on their song list. In 1965, the Who had their first U.S. hit single with "I Can't Explain," followed a year later by the powerful anthem "My Generation." From the beginning, however, the band established its reputation with its explosive live performances.

Onstage, the Who was a regular wrecking crew. Between verses, Daltrey twirled his microphone above his head like a lasso. Townshend leapt high in the air to begin his hard, rhythmic solos, attacking his guitar strings with the wide, circular motions of his arm. Drummer Keith Moon literally smashed his drums apart in the background as the set drew to a thunderous close, while Townshend banged his guitar to pieces against the stage floor and the speakers. Audiences were driven to a frenzy everywhere the band played, including a wildly energetic performance at 1969's Woodstock Music Festival.

That same year, the Who finally translated the success of its live performances into record sales with the release of the rock opera *Tommy*. Based on Townshend's recent conversion to the teachings of Meher Baba, an Indian religious leader, *Tommy* told the story of a "deaf, dumb and blind boy" who became a wizard at pinball. The double album reached number 10 on the charts, an achievement that would be matched or surpassed by all the band's subsequent recordings. In 1970, the Who released its finest studio recording, *Who's Next*, featuring the powerful, synthesizer-driven rock-and-roll anthems "Baba O'Reilly" and "We Don't Get Fooled Again."

The most successful of the harder-rocking blues-inspired British bands of the 1960s was the Rolling Stones. Lead singer Mick Jagger and guitarist Keith Richard had known each other as children in the London suburb of Dantford during the early 1950s. They had not seen each other for nearly a decade when Richard spotted his old friend one afternoon standing on a railroad platform with a stack of old blues and Chuck Berry recordings under his arm. Richard was an art student at the time, and Jagger was enrolled in the prestigious London School of Economics. After the two met young blues guitarist Brian Jones at a London club a few weeks later, they decided to drop out of school and form a band devoted to the music of their heroes, such as Berry, Little Richard, Muddy Waters, Howlin' Wolf, and Little Walter. Bass player Bill Wyman and drummer Charlie Watts were quickly recruited, along with the occasional support of pianist Ian Stewart. Within a few months, the Rolling Stones had become the best blues cover band in the early 1960s London underground.

In 1964, the Stones released their first top 10 single in the United States, the mournful but insistent "Time Is on My Side." Their first real recording milestone came the following year, however, when "(I Can't Get No) Satisfaction" began to climb the pop singles charts. After years of copying Chuck Berry riffs on guitar, Keith Richard had finally found a style that was his own. With its explosive guitar intro, controversial lyrics, and Jagger's desperate, pleading vocal, the song established the formula for the band's future success—as well as an ongoing problem with the censors.

If the Beatles caused controversy in the media and the music establishment, the Stones provoked outright hostility. With its sexually charged lyrics, "Satisfaction" was banned from airplay on many American radio stations, along with future Stones singles, such as "Let's Spend the Night Together." During the late 1960s, the band was tirelessly attacked by religious groups and the conservative press, and its members were closely watched and occasionally harassed by police in both England and the United States. The band members would not have had it any other way, however. They established their reputation during the mid-1960s by billing themselves as a darker, grittier alternative to the Beatles, and their problems on and off the stage only enhanced their appeal for many fans for whom the Beatles' music was too bright and optimistic. The band's haunting anthem, "Sympathy for the Devil," was a deliberate attempt to offend their harshest critics.

The Rolling Stones strike devilish poses in this publicity photo. The members of the band are: (seated, left to right) vocalist Mick Jagger, guitarist Brian Jones, and bassist Bill Wyman; (standing, left to right) guitarist Keith Richard and drummer Charlie Watts.

61

THE PRETTY THINGS

The Pretty Things may well be the most unfairly neglected band of the 1960s. Formed in 1963 by Phil May and Dick Taylor, who had earlier served a brief stint as the Rolling Stones' first bassist, the Pretty Things first made their mark as the loudest, meanest-looking, and ugliest-sounding hard rhythm-and-blues band in England. Like the Stones in England and the MC-5 in the United States, they played the kind of harsh, aggressive, sexually suggestive music that was designed to give rock and roll a bad name among parents, church leaders, and record company executives. They were also an extremely talented group of musicians, and their music, however loud and ugly, became stronger and more accessible with each new recording. Between the summers of 1964 and 1965, they released several top 20 singles in England, including "Don't Bring Me Down" and "Honey I Need."

As musical trends began to change in the second half of the 1960s, the Pretty Things changed with them. Beginning in 1967, their music took on an artier, more psychedelic edge on tunes like "Walking Through My Dreams," "Defecting Grey," and "Private Sorrow (A Phase in the Life of S. F. Sorrow)." After Dick Taylor left the band in 1969, the music became even odder and more experimental, and by the end of the decade, the Pretty Things had completely transformed themselves from the toughest, most uncompromising blues band on the British underground rock scene to the weirdest, trippiest band in British experimental rock. Although the later music never really caught on with the record-buying public, the band and its startlingly eclectic musical tastes became legendary among other rock musicians.

In 1969, the band's dark reputation took a tragically personal turn. Guitarist Brian Jones, who had recently been released from the band because of an ongoing problem with drugs, was found floating dead in the swimming pool of his London home. A few months later, a Stones fan was killed while the band performed at the Altamont Music Festival in San Francisco.

Between Jones's death and the tragedy at Altamont, the Stones released an album that finally placed them on par with the Beatles. In contrast to the youthful arrogance of their earlier recordings, 1969's "Let It Bleed" was a dark, brooding meditation on death, loneliness, and lost innocence. Among the album's several highlights were the gospel-tinged title cut; a slow, mournful version of blues legend Robert Johnson's "Love in Vain;" and "Country Honk," a loose, ragged treatment of the band's classic "Honky Tonk Women." Even more impressive were the hard-earned resignation of "You Can't Always Get What You Want" and the soulful urgency of Jagger's lead vocal on "Gimme Shelter."

Three years later, the band produced an even darker masterpiece, the double album *Exile on Main Street.* Though the album did not feature huge anthems like "Gimme Shelter" and "You Can't Always Get What You Want," it marked the band's full maturity as rock-and-roll musicians. Jagger, Richard, and the other band members had made the gospel-style shouting, the endlessly repeated blues riffs, the soulful background vocals, and the dark, jagged rhythms so fully their own that it had finally become impossible to tell where the influences ended and the band's original sound began. Not only was *Exile on Main Street* a great rock-and-roll recording, it was also a great blues recording.

5
BRINGING IT ALL BACK HOME

While the Beatles and the Rolling Stones were conquering the U.S. music charts, a small group of American musicians were producing new, intensely personal styles of music that would have an enormous impact on rock and roll throughout the remainder of the decade. The most gifted and unusual of this new wave of American rock-and-roll musicians were folk-rock pioneer Bob Dylan, Beach Boys composer Brian Wilson, and Frank Zappa, the outrageous composer and lead guitarist for the Mothers of Invention.

Bob Dylan was the most gifted and innovative composer to emerge from the folk music revival that swept across the United States and England during the early 1960s.

Times had been hard for folk musicians during the previous decade. For most of the 1950s, folk music, with its deep roots in the protest and labor movements, had been forced underground by pressure from anticommunist groups in the government, the media, and the record industry. In the early 1950s, the members of the nation's most popular folk group, the Weavers, suddenly found themselves without a record contract and with few opportunities to perform, only a couple of years after their single, "Goodnight,

Irene," had reached number one on the pop singles charts. The band's socially committed lead singer, Pete Seeger, spent much of the 1950s in England and Europe—along with other folk performers, like Ramblin' Jack Elliot, who were unable to find steady employment back in the United States. Even the great folk troubadour Woody Guthrie had trouble getting work during the period.

Things began to change, however, in 1958 when the San Francisco folk ensemble, the Kingston Trio, scored a surprise hit for Capitol Records with the traditional ballad "(Hang Down Your Head) Tom Dooley." As political tensions in the country began to relax, people became more receptive to folk songs, and music's association with left-wing and populist movements. Suddenly, folk artists around the country began signing recording contracts, playing in clubs, and appearing on the radio. By 1960, performers like Odetta, Theodore Bikel, Joan Baez, and Peter, Paul and Mary had begun to join the Kingston Trio on the record charts.

Things soon improved so much, in fact, that in the winter of 1961, Pete Seeger, just back from another successful tour of England, began to include protest songs in his concert repertoire. Seeger also began to write new songs about current social and political events. Younger artists followed Seeger's example, and by the summer of 1962, Peter, Paul and Mary's treatment of Seeger's cheerful protest anthem, "If I Had a Hammer," peaked at number two on the pop singles charts.

A gaunt, skinny kid with curly hair, deep-set eyes and a whiny, nasal tenor voice, Bob Dylan was an unlikely candidate to lead the folk music revival. Born Robert Zimmerman, Dylan renamed himself after the great Welsh lyric poet Dylan Thomas and began singing in rock-and-roll bands in his native Minnesota. His first love, however, was folk music, especially the smart, freewheeling tales sung by his idols, Woody Guthrie and Ramblin' Jack Elliot.

In January 1961, Dylan arrived in New York City, where he quickly became a favorite with the hip young audiences at the popular Greenwich Village folk music club, Gerdes' Folk City. Dylan was still struggling to find his own style as a composer, however. In his earliest performances in New York, he sang very few original tunes. Instead, he crouched awkwardly in front of the microphone, mumbling odd, irreverent versions of the traditional folk ballads he had learned from Guthrie, Elliot, and other older folk masters he had met along the way. In fact, Dylan's debut album, released that same year under the title *Bob Dylan*, was made up primarily of standard folk tunes, such as "In My Time of Dying," "Man of Constant Sorrow," and "The House of the Rising Sun."

In 1961, a young Bob Dylan earnestly sings a tune at the Bitter End, a New York City club.

A sharp-tongued, rebellious young man, Dylan soon established his reputation as a composer of protest songs. His next two albums, *The Times They Are A-Changin'* and *Freewheelin'*, were dominated by powerful, angry tunes against war, racism, and injustice. Some of Dylan's best songs from this period were "Blowin' in the Wind," "A Hard Rain's A-Gonna Fall," "Masters of War," "Oxford Town," and "The Times They Are A-Changin'." These recordings are now considered to be among the finest protest recordings ever made. During the next few years, Dylan's example would inspire countless folk and rock-and-roll musicians to write their own protest songs.

Dylan soon grew restless with his role as the voice of the protest movement. On his next recording, *Another Side of Bob Dylan*, he completely abandoned social concerns in favor of more personal, introspective material.

"There aren't any finger-pointing songs in here," he explained to a reporter at the time. "I don't want to write *for* people anymore—you know, be a spokesman. From now on I want to write from inside me."[26]

Dylan's decision to write personal ballads instead of protest songs was a controversial one within the folk community. Many people, especially the older musicians who had struggled for years to bring folk music back to the public, felt the strong-willed young singer had betrayed them. All this was nothing, however, compared to the excitement and controversy that Dylan would unleash with the release of his next album, *Bringing It All Back Home*. Recorded with a band full of rock-and-roll and blues musicians, the album featured loud, electric versions of Dylan's latest tunes. For folk purists, folk music and acoustic instruments were inseparable. Most folk stations refused to play Dylan's new electric songs for their listeners. But while many folk fans were offended by or lost interest in Dylan's music, young rock-and-roll fans were delighted by what they heard. *Bringing It All Back Home* quickly became Dylan's first recording to sell a million copies.

The most outrageous incident that resulted from Dylan's new sound occurred at the 1965 Newport Folk Festival in Rhode Island. Over the protest of many of the festival's organizers and participants, Dylan was allowed to perform a set with some of the rock-and-roll musicians featured on his new album. From the first note, it was almost impossible to hear the band's explosive performance above the chorus of boos that came from the traditional folk fans in the audience—and the screaming and applause of the younger rock-and-roll contingent. Backstage, a fight actually broke out between the usually gentle-mannered Pete Seeger, who was determined to unplug the band's equipment and end the concert, and one of the stagehands. While Dylan provoked the crowd with electric versions of his most-admired folk tunes, the two men wrestled together on the backstage floor.

Dylan followed the success of *Bringing It All Back Home* with two of the finest recordings of the rock-and-roll era: *Highway 61 Revisited* and *Blonde on Blonde*. He also released the period's most powerful and influential rock-and-roll single, "Like a Rolling Stone." In just two years, Dylan had completely remade himself from a folk troubadour to a rock idol. He had also become the one American rock-and-roll composer whom even the Beatles and the Rolling Stones held in awe.

During this period, Dylan began touring with a talented young folk-rock ensemble known as the Hawks. Renamed as the Band, the group would later emerge as one of the most respected rock-and-roll acts of the late 1960s and early 1970s.

Dylan soon became restless again, however, and he completely lost interest in being a rock-and-roll star. Following a serious motorcycle accident in the spring of 1967, he went into seclusion for almost a year. In spite of the interest and concern of his fans, he stopped both recording and performing live during the period and refused to have any contact with the media. When he did return to music in 1968, Dylan had remodeled himself once again, this time as a country musician.

"I thought I was just gonna get up and go back to doing what I was doing before," Dylan explained to *Rolling Stone* editor Jann Wenner regarding his decision to leave rock and roll, "but I couldn't do it anymore."[27] In place of the rock-and-roll fury of "Like a Rolling Stone," Dylan's next two albums, *John Wesley Harding* and *Nashville Skyline,* featured lazy country ballads like "Lay Lady Lay" and "Tonight I'll Be Staying Here with You." On the latter album's "Girl from the North Country," Dylan even sang an off-beat and slightly off-key duet with country music star Johnny Cash.

But Dylan had already made a lasting impression on rock and roll. In the years that followed, performers like the Byrds, the Band, and the Jimi Hendrix Experience would introduce his songs to new listeners, and countless rock-and-roll bands would find inspiration from the brilliant, uncompromising example of his electric recordings from the mid-1960s.

While Bob Dylan's music reminded young people in the early 1960s that they were part of a larger social world full of suffering and injustice, the Beach Boys sang as if nothing could possibly be more important than a sunny day at the beach.

Formed in 1961 by Brian Wilson and his cousin Mike Love, the band also included Brian's younger brothers, Dennis and Carl, and Al Jardine, a high school classmate from the boys' hometown of Hawthorne, California.

From the group's beginning, Brian was the band leader and songwriter. Shy, introverted, and given to periods of depression,

Brian wrote songs about an endless California summer vacation, in which dating, surfing, and drag racing were the main events.

The Beach Boys were never very proficient on their instruments and would eventually recruit professional session musicians to fill out their thin, twangy sound in concert. But it was the band's vocal, not their instrumental, performances that made them special. All of them sang beautifully, especially when they were singing together. Brian filled the group's songs with tight, complex harmonies that made the Beach Boys sound more like angels than beach bums.

Although most of them lived nowhere near the ocean or a beach, teenagers all across the United States were captivated by Brian's bright, cheerful anthems to teenage life, such as "Surfer Girl," "Little Deuce Coup," "Surfin' U.S.A.," and "Surf City." Brian co-wrote the latter tune with Jan Berry of Jan and Dean, one of the numerous vocal groups inspired by the Beach Boys' success. In little more than a year after they formed, the Beach Boys became the most popular band in the country, and surf music became a nationwide phenomenon.

"He worked a loose-limbed group sound and added his own falsetto," wrote rock critic Nick Cohn of Wilson's extraordinary gifts as a songwriter and the band's uncanny ability to capture the entire nation's imagination. "Then he stuck in some lazy twangy guitars and rounded it all out with jumped-up Four Freshmen harmonies. No sweat, he'd created a bona fide surf music out of nothing. More, he had invented California."[28]

Everywhere one looked in the early 1960s, there were beach movies, beach television programs, and beach parties, complete with truckloads of sand hauled in just for the occasion. And beach music, especially the Beach Boys' music, provided a nonstop soundtrack for it all.

The Beach Boys—(clockwise from top) Brian Wilson, Carl Wilson, Mike Love, Al Jardine, and Dennis Wilson—pose for an early publicity

As the Beach Boys became more successful, however, Brian began to suffer from depression and violent mood swings. Always shy and withdrawn, he found the demands of performing live with the band and traveling back and forth across the country to be incredibly stressful. Finally, in 1964, the pressure became too much for him, and on an airplane flight to a Beach Boys concert in Hous-

71

ton, Texas, he suffered the first of what would be many nervous breakdowns. "His face first went red as a beetroot," a witness would later report to British journalist Nick Kent, "and then it turned deathly white and he started screaming he was going to die, before breaking down and crying like a little baby."[29]

Brian soon recovered from the episode, but he had several more breakdowns during the next few months and finally decided to stop touring with the band altogether. While this weakened the band's sound in concert—Brian sang lead on many of their more popular songs—it also gave him much more time to devote to songwriting and to producing the band's recordings in the studio.

By the end of 1963, the Beatles had replaced the Beach Boys as the most popular band in America. Brian was determined to put his band back on top, however, and he spent countless hours writing new tunes and remixing the band's studio recordings. "Generally I was a perfectionist," Brian later confessed to Nick Kent, "that went into the studio with a certain amount of panic in my chest. The fear of being rejected drove me to be doing something which was pretty good. Those Beatles guys totally stole the limelight. They stole the show in the recording business, and with the public."[30]

Finally, in the summer of 1966, the Beach Boys released *Pet Sounds*. The recording failed to reestablish the Beach Boys as the number-one band in the country, but it did mark the emergence of Brian Wilson as one of the most gifted and daring composers and producers of his generation. From start to finish, the album featured a level of orchestration and electronic effects that had never before been heard on a rock-and-roll recording. There were lush string arrangements, pounding bass drums, and so many layers of vocals that Brian's frail tenor voice sounded at times like an entire choir.

In addition to all the musical advances, *Pet Sounds* also signaled a change in Brian's lyrics, which had become much more personal and introspective in the year and a half since he had stopped performing live with the band. There were still plenty of songs about dating and life at the beach on the new recording, such as the hit singles "Wouldn't It Be Nice" and "Sloop John B." What really set the album apart from virtually everything else on the radio, however, were several deeply personal numbers about loneliness and insecurity, such as "I Know There's an Answer" and "I Guess I Just Wasn't Made for These Times." The latter song featured Brian's anguished schoolboy confession, "They say I got brains, but they ain't doin' me no good." On the song's chorus, Brian repeated the phrase, "Sometimes I feel very sad," over and over, while the rest of the band harmonized on what sounded like the vocal equivalent of a trombone fanfare.

Pet Sounds was completely unexpected from a band that had built its reputation singing about fast cars and sun-drenched beaches. Although the album may not have forced the Beatles off the top of the charts, it did earn the British band's attention and respect. According to one report, John Lennon and Paul McCartney rushed home after first hearing *Pet Sounds* to write the beautiful ballad "Here, There and Everywhere."[31] During the next few years, *Pet Sounds* would be the standard against which the Beatles and other artists would measure the quality of their own recordings.

Brian was far from satisfied by the recording's modest commercial success, however, or the numerous positive reviews the record received from the press. As soon as *Pet Sounds* was completed, he began working on an even more ambitious project. By the time Brian finished the single "Good Vibrations," he had spent more than six months and $16,000 on the song, more than three times the cost of a normal rock-and-roll *album* at the time. Despite doubts among some executives at MGM, the band's record company, that such an intricate and complex recording would be well-received on the radio, "Good Vibrations" immediately became a hit. Inspired by the song's success, Brian teamed up with another young, offbeat Los Angeles composer, Van Dyke Parks, to produce an entire Beach Boys album that he hoped would be as complex and demanding as "Good Vibrations."

Smile, as Brian planned to call the album, was doomed from the beginning. Brian's music for the project was brilliant, and some of the recording sessions, especially the early takes on "Surf's Up" and "Cabin Essence," showed promise that Brian actually might be able to complete his masterpiece. But along with the creative bursts came violent mood swings and lengthy periods of depression. Like many other rock-and-roll musicians at the time, Brian had begun to experiment heavily with drugs, and this made his behavior even more unpredictable than before. Sometimes he would suddenly stop singing in the middle of a session and burst into laughter. At other times, he was simply too depressed to work at all. When Brian discovered that a neighbor's home had been badly burned in a fire, he became so upset that he set fire to the tapes that he and the band had spent the previous day recording.

The band's recording label had been hesitant to fund the recording even before Brian's breakdown. By this time, everyone involved in the project could tell that Brian was in no condition to finish what he had started, and plans for the completion of *Smile* were canceled. A few of the songs from the sessions would be released in less-ambitious form the following year on the album *Smiley Smile*. Brian and the Beach Boys would also make several other fine albums together during the remainder of the decade, including *Wild Honey* and *Surf's Up*. But the band would never again approach the level of quality and innovation that they had achieved on *Pet Sounds* and "Good Vibrations."

Eventually conflicts within the band and his own continuing problems with depression would cause Brian to leave the band. In the 1970s, the Beach Boys would be reduced to performing their old surf hits at rock-and-roll revivals. *Pet Sounds*, however, remains one of rock and roll's true classics, and Brian Wilson's music continues to inspire each new generation of rock-and-roll composers and performers.

No matter how daring or unconventional his music became, Brian Wilson continued to think of himself as a rock-and-roll musician. His greatest ambition was always to be more popular than the Beatles. Even his oddest and most innovative songs were populated with normal teenagers with fast cars, broken hearts, and an endless love for the beach. The same cannot be said, however, for one of Wilson's older and more influential contemporaries in the mid-1960s Los Angeles music scene.

Frank Zappa, the brilliantly offbeat composer and mastermind of the Mothers of Invention, never thought of himself as a rock-and-roll performer. He cared very little what the Beatles or anyone else thought of his music. Born in Baltimore, Maryland, during the Christmas holidays of 1940, Francis Vincent Zappa Jr. was the oldest child of Greek and Italian immigrants. Even before he grew the big, looping mustache and shoulder-length hair that he would wear throughout most of his adult life, Zappa was already a goofy-looking kid who found himself at odds with the rest of the world. Tall and lanky, he had deep, piercing eyes, a sharp, hooked nose, and a quick wit and rebellious attitude that frequently got him kicked out of school or beaten up by the tougher kids in the neighborhood.

When Frank was 10 years old, the family moved to the small town of Lancaster, California. Lancaster was in the middle of the Mojave Desert, two hours east of Los Angeles by car. In Lancaster, Frank met other similarly rebellious spirits, including Don Van

Vliet, who would later be known to rock-and-roll fans as Captain Beefheart. Van Vliet introduced Zappa to the dark, intense music of the blues, including the songs of Robert Johnson and Howlin' Wolf, and the louder, more danceable tunes of rhythm and blues.

"In those days," Zappa would later recall, "I was a rhythm and blues fanatic. I was extremely suspect of any rock played by white people."[32]

Soon Frank purchased a cheap electric guitar, joined a local dance band, and began playing rhythm-and-blues standards in the sleazy Latino beer halls and strip joints around Lancaster.

Zappa's first love, however, was for more serious music, the kind that made you think instead of dance. As a teenager, he was inspired by the compositions of Igor Stravinsky and Edgar Varese. Stravinsky was an early-twentieth-century classical composer from Russia with a rare gift for the use of rhythm in his compositions and a playful relationship with the classical music of the past. Varese, who was still alive when the 13-year-old Zappa first discovered his music, was one of the earliest composers to use tapes and electronic effects in his work.

Varese's music was made even more appealing to Zappa by the fact that one of the composer's more recent works was called "Deserts." "This thrilled me quite a lot," remembered Zappa years later, "because I was living in Lancaster, California at the time. When you're fifteen and living in the Mojave Desert and find out that the world's greatest composer is working on a song about your 'home town,' you can get pretty excited."[33]

After finishing high school, Zappa moved to Los Angeles, where he continued to play in bands while also trying to make his mark as a composer for motion pictures using the techniques he had learned from Stravinsky and Varese. During the early 1960s, he wrote the sound tracks for two low-budget films, *Run Home*

Slow and *The World's Greatest Sinner*. But with his increasingly unconventional appearance and behavior, Zappa found himself becoming more and more a part of Los Angeles's rock-and-roll-oriented youth movement. In 1964, he auditioned as the lead guitarist for a local rhythm-and-blues band called the Soul Giants. The other band members—singer Ray Collins, drummer Jim Black, bass player Roy Estrada, and rhythm guitarist Elliot Ingberger—shared Zappa's serious musical ambitions and weird sense of humor. Within a few months, Zappa had become the group's leader, renaming them the Mothers of Invention and replacing their normal repertoire of rock-and-roll and rhythm-and-blues standards with his own offbeat compositions. Although the band was often booed off the stage during their early performances, Zappa remained convinced that success was always just around the corner.

"Okay, you guys," he told the other band members, "I've got this plan. We are going to get rich. You probably won't believe it now, but if you just bear with me, we'll go out and do it."[34]

By the end of the year, Zappa and the Mothers of Invention were playing regularly at the Whiskey-a-Go-Go, Los Angeles's most popular rock-and-roll club. Following one of the Mothers' shows at the Whiskey, two representatives of MGM Records, Herb Cohen and Tom Wilson, approached Zappa to offer the band a recording contract.

Released early in 1966, the band's debut, *Freak Out*, was as groundbreaking as it was bizarre. The entire recording revolved around the long-haired, colorfully dressed Los Angeles youth culture who called themselves "freaks." Inspired by Stravinsky, Zappa exhibited a playful attitude toward all types of music on the recording. There were obvious references to the Beatles, the Rolling Stones, doo-wop, rhythm and blues, jazz, and even a few brief snatches of symphonic music. Also inspired by Varese, Zappa used overdubbing and various electronic effects to bring all the different sounds and styles of music together.

By the time Zappa had finished *Freak Out*, he had managed to spend $25,000 of MGM's money—more than five times the cost of most recordings—and to fill four full sides of vinyl. This made the Mothers' debut recording the first double rock-and-roll album.

Freak Out was a huge success for the band, and before long, young people around the country were calling themselves freaks and searching for opportunities to "freak out." Zappa soon made it clear, however, that he had no intention of starting a youth movement. He simply wanted to encourage people to act as individuals. The Mothers' next two albums, *Absolutely Free* and *We're Only in It for the Money*, were full of lyrics condemning the mindless conformity of the freak and hippie movements. Other recordings, such as *Uncle Meat* and Zappa's solo project, *Lumpy Gravy*, were so strange and unsettling that Zappa actually seemed to be trying to scare his fans away.

By the end of 1970, the original Mothers of Invention had broken up, and everyone, including Zappa, was bitter that the band had never lived up to its promise. Zappa would soon form a new version of the Mothers, with whom he would continue to perform and record for more than a decade.

Zappa's finest achievements, however, would come outside the band. The first was as a producer for Captain Beefheart's extraordinary double album, *Trout Mask Replica*. With its jerky stop-and-start rhythms, offbeat lyrics, and Beefheart's bluesy, five-octave vocals, the album is one of the strangest rock-and-roll albums ever made. Zappa's imaginative production kept things just clean and ordered enough to make sense.

Zappa's other triumph during the period was the 1969 solo album *Hot Rats*. The album featured violinist Jean-Luc Ponty and

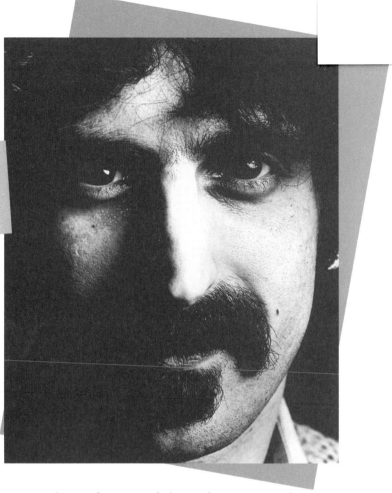

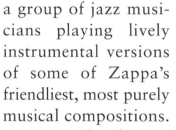
Frank Zappa, pictured here in 1975, was one of rock and roll's most eccentric composers.

a group of jazz musicians playing lively instrumental versions of some of Zappa's friendliest, most purely musical compositions. *Hot Rats* also featured a number of powerful performances by Zappa himself, and a tough, throaty vocal by Captain Beefheart on the album's one strictly rock-and-roll number, "Willie the Pimp." Released at a time when free-form instrumental jams dominated rock-and-roll recordings, "*Hot Rats*," wrote *Rolling Stone* critic Lester Bangs at the time, could "whale the tar out of every other informal jam released in rock and roll for the past two years."[35] Loud, expansive, and full of life, *Hot Rats* was the one Frank Zappa album that could actually make you think and dance at the same time.

6
CROSSROADS

The influence of the blues continued to play an important role in rock and roll during the second half of the 1960s. A new wave of British bands, like the Yardbirds and Ten Years After, and American bands, such as the Electric Flag and the Allman Brothers, introduced teenage music fans to the big-guitar sound of urban, Chicago-style blues. These blues-inspired bands also introduced a new style of performance and improvisation that would dominate rock-and-roll concerts and recordings throughout the remainder of the decade.

The most prominent figure of late-1960s blues-influenced rock and roll was British guitarist Eric Clapton. Clapton began his career in the early 1960s as a rhythm-and-blues guitarist, playing briefly in two unsigned bands, the Roosters and Casey Jones and the Engineers. He soon lost interest in rhythm and blues, however, abandoning performing for a couple of years to study the guitar techniques of blues masters like Robert Johnson, Skip James, Big Bill Broonzy, and Blind Boy Fuller.

"I just finally got completely overwhelmed in this brand new world," the guitarist would later explain. "I studied it and listened to it and went right down in it. When I came back up in it, [I got] turned on to B. B. King and it's been that way ever since."[36]

The most spectacular of the Mississippi Delta blues guitarists during the mid-1950s, King transformed the electric guitar into the centerpiece of the blues ensemble. In his live performances, King thrilled his mostly African-American audiences with huge, arching guitar solos that often completely overwhelmed the songs that supported them.

Still in his teens when he first heard King's recordings, Clapton was determined to transplant the Delta musician's big, improvisational guitar style into a rock-and-roll setting. During the mid-1960s, Clapton spent brief periods with two blues-inspired English rock-and-roll bands, John Mayall's Blues Breakers and the Yardbirds. But Mayall's band was far too traditional for Clapton's taste, and the Yardbirds were too concerned with producing hit records. Clapton was interested in something much more experimental. He wanted to find a way to improvise for rock-and-roll fans in the same way that B. B. King improvised for his fans on the blues circuit.

In 1966, Clapton joined with blues-rock bass player Jack Bruce and the more jazz-influenced drummer Ginger Baker to form the rock-and-roll trio Cream. Both Baker and Bruce had played for the blues-inspired Graham Bond Organization during the early 1960s, and Clapton and Bruce had played briefly together for Mayall's Blues Breakers in 1965.

On their studio recordings, Cream was uneven at best, combining hard, aggressive covers of blues standards, such as Robert Johnson's "Crossroads" and Skip James's "I'm So Glad," with their own offbeat, drug-inspired tunes. In concert, however, Clapton's new band created a sound unlike anything anyone had ever heard before. Three-minute tunes were frequently expanded into 20- to

Cream—(from left to right) guitarist Eric Clapton, bassist Jack Bruce, and drummer Ginger Baker—pose backstage during their 1966 tour.

30-minute improvisations, with all three musicians leaving the original melody and rhythm far behind. Cream was also thunderously loud in performance, and Clapton's high, piercing guitar solos left early audiences completely in awe. Many British fans were so impressed, in fact, that they began to inscribe the slogan "Clapton is God" on subway walls.

By the time of the band's second release, *Disraeli Gears*, Cream had become a musical phenomenon in the United States as well. All of the band's remaining albums reached *Billboard*'s top ten, and their 1968 double album, *Wheels of Fire*, climbed all the way to number one on the charts.

Successful recordings meant very little to Clapton, however. When Cream began to lose its spontaneity in concert toward the end of 1968, Clapton left the band at the height of its popularity. He would soon reunite briefly with Baker to form the psychedelic blues ensemble Blind Faith, along with Traffic's lead singer and keyboardist, Steve Winwood.

At the end of the decade, Clapton spent several months jamming informally and touring the American South with the gospel-influenced rock-and-roll collective Delaney and Bonnie and Friends. The guitarist's work with Delaney and Bonnie, on 1970's "Delaney and Bonnie on Tour with Eric Clapton," had a sweet, lyrical quality that he had never displayed on any of his previous recordings. His new playing was much closer to the haunting country blues techniques of Skip James and Robert Johnson than the louder, more aggressive urban blues style he had used with Cream.

Later in the year, Clapton formed the band Derek and the Dominoes. The band's first album, *Layla* (1970), successfully combined the cleaner, more lyrical quality of the guitarist's recent performances with the loud, furious style of Cream. *Layla* also gave Clapton the chance to perform with the great slide guitarist Duane Allman, of the Allman Brothers, who overdubbed a second lead guitar on several of the album's tracks. With rousing blues anthems, such as "Bell Bottom Blues" and "Why Does Love Got to Be So Sad," the album turned out to be Clapton's most perfect recording and one of the finest rock-and-roll recordings ever made. After almost a decade of experimenting with blues standards, Clapton had finally found a way to write and record his own unique style of blues-inspired rock and roll.

Los Angeles's the Doors was another late-1960s band to

experiment with the blues. Unlike Clapton and Cream, however, the Doors and their darkly handsome, charismatic lead singer Jim Morrison were more concerned with the darker, more confessional side of the blues than the big-guitar sound used by Cream.

A film student at UCLA, Morrison formed the Doors in 1966, along with guitarist Robby Krieger, drummer John Densmore, and Ray Manzarek on organ. From the beginning, Morrison was the band leader, writing dark, brooding songs about drugs, death, and forbidden sexual desire. The other band members brought Morrison's tunes to life with harsh, jerky instrumental arrangements that sometimes sounded more like a drunken circus band than a rock-and-roll group.

Even before they released their first album, *The Doors* (1967), Morrison and the band were creating a stir in the hip Los Angeles clubs where they performed, such as the Whiskey-a-Go-Go. Onstage, Morrison was a shouting, swirling rock-and-roll shaman. Whenever the mood struck him, he would interrupt a song to make a personal confession or lecture the audience about their drab, conventional lives. Just as quickly, he would be singing again, down on his knees with the microphone pressed tightly to his lips with the band's high-pitched music exploding behind him.

Occasionally, both Morrison and his audience got a little out of control. The police were frequently called in to restrain the crowd, and the singer was arrested on several occasions for public obscenity and indecent exposure.

"Sometimes, I'll extend myself and work people up a bit," he told an interviewer in 1967, "but usually we're out there trying to make good music and that's it. Each time it's different. There are varying degrees of fever in the auditorium waiting for you. So you go out on stage and you're met with this rush of energy potential. You never know what it's going to be."[37]

Released by Elektra Records, the Doors' 1967 debut was an immediate sensation. On hard, driving tunes like "Light My Fire" and "Break on Through," the band successfully translated onto vinyl the fury and energy of their live performances. By the end of the year, the album had peaked at number two on the album charts. It took the Beatles' *Sgt. Pepper's Lonely Hearts Club Band* to keep it from reaching number one.

Over the next three years, the Doors would release several successful albums, along with hit singles like "Hello, I Love You" and "Riders on the Storm." By the end of the decade, however, legal problems and Morrison's own personal demons had ended the band's touring days. Depressed, overweight, and with a serious drinking problem, Morrison devoted most of his time to writing and recording his own highly personal poetry. On July 3, 1971, Morrison died suddenly of a heart attack in a Paris hotel room.

While Morrison and the Doors were stirring up crowds in Los Angeles, a few hundred miles up the Pacific coast, a number of bands were developing something known as the San Francisco sound. The new bands combined the blues-oriented rock and roll of Clapton and the Doors with lighter, airier instrumental techniques borrowed from traditional folk and country music. It was more than musical influences, however, that made the San Francisco sound so distinctive.

During the 1960s, a number of radical, avant-garde movements converged in the San Francisco Bay area. The student "free speech" movement had started across the bay at the University of California at Berkeley earlier in the decade. Many of the major "beat" poets and writers, such as Gregory Corso, Lawrence Ferlinghetti, and Ken Kesey, made their home in the city. Now, thousands of young hippies—with their long hair, bright clothes, and endless supply of drugs—began to crowd into a small neighborhood near the city's Golden Gate Park known as Haight-Ashbury.

The new San Francisco bands were very much a part of this exciting new youth culture. Their unique style of performance, known as psychedelic rock, reflected the spirit of freedom and experimentation that had swept over the entire community. More than anything else, psychedelic rock was influenced by the unprecedented amount of drugs that young people in the area were consuming. San Francisco bands like Country Joe and the Fish, Quicksilver Messenger Service, Big Brother and the Holding Company, and the Jefferson Airplane made music that conveyed the mellowness, bright hallucinations, and occasionally dark, disturbing side effects associated with marijuana, hashish, LSD, and other drugs.

With its tight, aggressive rhythm section, Quicksilver Messenger Service was the closest thing the Bay Area had to a hard, straightforward rock-and-roll dance band. On the more folk-oriented side, the Jefferson Airplane and Country Joe and the Fish wrote tough, uncompromising protest songs, such as the Airplane's "Volunteers" and Country Joe McDonald's "I Feel Like I'm Fixin' to Die Rag." Big Brother and the Holding Company introduced San Francisco youth to a harder, blues-oriented style of rock and roll. The band's extraordinary lead singer, Janis Joplin, had a powerful but vulnerable vocal style that impressed even jazz and blues followers outside the rock-and-roll community. Until her death from a drug overdose on October 4, 1970, Joplin would reign as the most respected female vocalist in rock and roll.

The most enduring band to come out of the late-1960s San Francisco music scene was the Grateful Dead. Led by country- and jazz-influenced lead guitarist Jerry Garcia, the Dead, more than any other band, embodied the free, experimental spirit of the Bay Area youth movement—both in their music and their behavior off the stage. During the late 1960s, the band members lived together in an old Victorian house near the corner of Haight and Ashbury, the two streets from which their neighborhood got its name.

The Grateful Dead loved to play their music live, whenever and wherever they got the chance. Their favorite venue was in the Golden Gate Park, just a few blocks down Haight Street from their communal home. They usually played for free, in spontaneous, unannounced jams that often lasted for hours. The Dead's open concerts in the park soon became the basis for regular "happenings" or "be-ins," featuring poets, musicians, jugglers, and other rock musicians in all-day festivals of music and performance art.

Like Cream, the Grateful Dead were never quite able to capture the excitement of their live performances in their studio recordings. Their best album from the period, *Workingman's Dead* (1970), featured a pleasant assortment of original folk- and country-style ballads. There was no attempt whatsoever to duplicate the type of extended instrumental jams that made up so much of their concerts.

It was the instrumental jams, however, that the fans loved the most. In fact, some of the Dead's listeners were so impressed with the band's live shows, which normally lasted for at least four hours, that they became almost fanatical in their enthusiasm, following the band across the country in order to attend every show on their tours. Calling themselves Deadheads, the Dead's worldwide following would eventually make the band the most popular live act in the history of rock and roll. Until Garcia's death in 1995, the Grateful Dead would continue to fill stadiums and large concert halls wherever they went.

Toward the end of 1967, San Francisco would make another significant contribution to rock-and-roll culture when Jann Wenner, a young rock journalist, and the respected jazz critic Ralph J. Gleason published the first issue of *Rolling Stone*. Not only did the new magazine allow young people to read up-to-date reviews and interviews with new musicians like Jim Morrison, Janis Joplin, Frank Zappa, and John Lennon. Along with other new or soon-to-be-formed magazines, like *Creem*, *Fusion*, and *Crawdaddy*, it also gave thousands of young people who lived outside such music centers as New York and San Francisco a chance to learn about and feel a part of the new rock-and-roll culture.

The most spectacularly gifted rock-and-roll musician to emerge during the late 1960s was guitarist Jimi Hendrix. Born in Seattle, Washington, in 1942, Hendrix began playing in local rhythm-and-blues and rock-and-roll bands, like the Rocking Kings, while he was still in high school. By the time he dropped out of school to join the Air Force paratroopers in 1960, he had already become the best rock guitarist in the Seattle area. Hendrix's first love was the blues, however, from the imaginative lead techniques of Robert Johnson and Elmore James to the darker, more subtle rhythms of Robert Lockwood Jr. and Billy Butler.

In the Air Force, Hendrix spent every free minute practicing his guitar. He became so obsessed with developing his technique that he started taking his guitar to bed with him. He hoped that—like the great blues guitarist Mississippi John Hurt—he could somehow learn to practice in his sleep. To the amusement of his fellow paratroopers, and the concern of his superiors, he even began to talk affectionately to his guitar. Like another blues idol, B. B. King, he also gave his instrument a name, Betty Jean, which he painted in big bold letters on its back.

Eventually, Hendrix's unusual behavior led to a discharge from the Air Force and a reunion with the Seattle rock-and-roll scene. Hendrix's technique had improved so much during his stay in the military that he quickly became a musical phenomenon in

Seattle. Soon he was attracting the attention of the more established musicians who passed through the area on tour.

Hendrix finally got his big break when Little Richard invited him to play guitar in his touring band. The job with Little Richard lasted less than a year, however. The vain, quick-tempered band leader eventually kicked his young guitarist off the tour for his flamboyant clothing and stage manner, and his frequent failure to show up for performances. But Hendrix had already proved his worth as a rhythm guitarist, and he spent the next couple of years playing for a number of leading rhythm-and-blues ensembles, including the Isley Brothers, Curtis Knight and the Squires, and King Curtis.

After a few months in New York City, playing guitar in a progressive blues band called Jimmy James and the Blue Flames, Hendrix traveled to England in 1966. Almost immediately after his arrival, he formed a new band along with bass player Noel Redding and drummer Mitch Mitchell. Within a few months, the Jimi Hendrix Experience was one of the most popular bands in England, sharing the same stage with major artists like Eric Clapton and the Who. By the time Hendrix signed a deal to make albums for Reprise Records in the spring of 1967, the band's singles, "Hey Joe" and "Purple Haze," had already reached the top of the British charts.

Hendrix and his band made their U.S. debut at the Monterey Pop Festival in California that same spring, followed by a national tour with the Monkees. The Monkees were the most popular U.S. band at the time and the stars of their own prime-time television program. By the time the tour ended, Hendrix and his band had more than equaled their success in England. Their albums—*Are You Experienced?* (1967), *Axis: Bold as Love* (1968), *Electric Ladyland* (1968), and *Smash Hits* (1969)—would approach the top of the *Billboard* charts.

Guitar-god Jimi Hendrix bends some mean notes on his Stratocaster. Hendrix's innovative guitar style changed the sound of rock and roll.

Like Clapton and the Grateful Dead, however, it was in concert that Hendrix caused the biggest stir. Using tricks he had learned from blues masters like Guitar Slim and T-Bone Walker, he would thrill young audiences by playing the guitar with his teeth or behind his head. At the end of the set, he sometimes smashed his instrument to pieces right before the crowd, then soaked it in lighter fluid and set it on fire.

Along with his outrageous behavior on stage, Hendrix also impressed crowds with the remarkable sounds he could coax out of his guitar. Using hammered strings, carefully controlled feedback, and unorthodox chordings, he created a roaring, furious guitar style that was simultaneously rhythm and lead, both deafeningly loud and imaginatively melodic.

"He uses an immense vocabulary of controlled sounds," explained guitarist Mike Bloomfield at the time, "not just hoping to get those sounds, but actually controlling them as soon as he produces them. I have never heard such controlled frenzy, especially in electric music."[38]

Toward the end of the decade, Hendrix left the Experience to form a more blues-influenced ensemble. Known as the Band of Gypsies, the band included drummer Buddy Miles and bass player Billy Cox, an old friend of Hendrix's from the Air Force. The trio released the live album, *Band of Gypsies*, in 1970.

Hendrix's finest moment came in the summer of 1969 when he received top billing and performed as the final act at the Woodstock Music Festival. The three-day event brought more than 300,000 rock-and-roll fans peacefully together on a small farm just outside of Woodstock, New York. In addition to Hendrix's inspired performance, which included a huge, explosive version of "The Star-Spangled Banner," Woodstock featured many of rock and roll's top acts. Among the highlights were performances by the Jefferson Airplane, Creedence Clearwater Revival, the Grateful Dead, the Who, Janis Joplin, Sly and the Family Stone, and Crosby, Stills, Nash and Young.

The positive feelings generated by Woodstock were short-lived, however. A few months later, in December 1969, another huge music festival outside San Francisco produced tragically different results. More than 300,000 music fans crowded into the Altamont Raceway to hear bands like the Grateful Dead, the Jefferson Airplane, and the Rolling Stones. Toward the end of the day, while the Stones were performing their dark classic, "Sympathy for the Devil," a disturbance broke out near the front of the stage. During a scuffle involving several members of the Hell's Angels, the motorcycle club that the Stones had hired to guard the stage, a man in the audience named Meredith Hunter suddenly pulled a gun from his coat. One of the Hell's Angels pulled out a knife and stabbed the man to death before he had a chance to fire.

By the time the city's sanitation workers had begun clearing off the speedway the next morning, news of the tragedy had spread around the world. The optimism and euphoria generated by Woodstock had suddenly come to an end.

A few months later in London, on September 18, 1970, Jimi Hendrix died suddenly from complications following an overdose of sleeping pills. He was 27 years old.

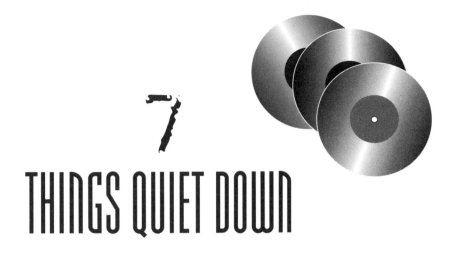

7
THINGS QUIET DOWN

After the breakup of the Beatles and the tragedy of Altamont, the rock-and-roll community suddenly found itself without a common identity. Fans of Jimi Hendrix, the Doors, and the Grateful Dead may have differed in terms of their musical tastes, but everyone agreed that rock and roll was a powerful force in society. During the late 1960s, most rock-and-roll fans believed that music could be used to fight racism and injustice, to stop the Vietnam War, and to help young people build a vital new community in which friendship, love, and free expression were more important than money, power, and war.

As the decade drew to a close, however, most young people were far less confident in what rock and roll could do and far less excited about coming together as a group at big events like Woodstock and Altamont. More and more, small clubs and concert halls became the favorite place of many young fans to listen to music, and soft, introspective, intensely personal folk songs began to replace hard, aggressive protest songs as the most popular music of the day.

Folk music had maintained a degree of popularity during the 1960s. Since Dylan's controversial break with protest music on *Another Side*, artists like Joan Baez, Tim Hardin, Phil Ochs, Leonard Cohen, Tim Buckley, and Simon and Garfunkel had continued to provide young people with a steady stream of quality recordings. In major cities throughout the nation, these artists continued to play regularly in tiny, smoke-filled clubs for a small but loyal following. In early 1970, however, folk music began to reassert itself as one of the most popular forms of music for young rock-and-roll fans everywhere.

The most popular of the new rock-inspired folk singers was James Taylor. The North Carolina singer-songwriter had been making a name for himself since the mid-1960s playing his quiet, contemplative songs in the small bars and coffee houses around McDougal Street in Manhattan's Greenwich Village. In 1968, the Beatles were so impressed with one of Taylor's performances that they recruited him as the first new act to be recorded on their newly formed Apple Records. Taylor's debut recording, *The Flying Machine*, attracted little attention outside the regular folk community. Things went differently for his second album, however. Released by Warner Brothers Records early in 1970, *Sweet Baby James* quickly became one of the most successful pop recordings of the year. The album's immediate success inspired a rebirth of interest in singer-songwriter-style folk-rock.

Like Bob Dylan before him, the tall, lanky Taylor sang his songs in a high, nasal whine. Unlike his great folk predecessor, however, Taylor had extremely limited gifts as a songwriter. Most of his tunes repeated the same themes of loneliness, lost innocence, and guilt—and a constant longing for the cozy childhood home that his own restless spirit had caused him to leave behind. To many hard-core rock-and-roll fans, Taylor's songs were silly, self-

94

pitying, and pretentious and had little in common with the folk and blues traditions that inspired them. During the early 1970s, Taylor became a favorite target of the rock-and-roll press, who frequently criticized the young folk singer and the new style of soft rock that he had inspired. One of the angriest and funniest attacks came from rock critic Lester Bangs. In 1971, Bangs interrupted one of his lengthy reviews to describe a murderous fantasy involving Taylor. In Bangs's fantasy, the rock critic imagined himself traveling all the way from California to North Carolina by bus to kill the nasal-voiced folk singer with a broken wine bottle and put an end to folk-rock once and for all.

"EXTRA!" proclaimed an imagined *Rolling Stone* news headline toward the end of Bangs's piece. "TRAGEDY STRIKES ROCK! SUPERSTAR GORED BY DERANGED ROCK CRITIC! 'We made it,' gasped Lester Bangs as he was led by police from the scene. 'We won.' "[39]

Despite the hostility of Bangs and other rock critics, most young people loved Taylor's soft confessional style of folk-rock. Within 12 months of the release of *Sweet Baby James*, gifted songwriters like Joni Mitchell, Neil Young, and Paul Simon had all released successful and critically acclaimed solo recordings.

For years, Simon and his partner Art Garfunkel had worked together as a duo, enjoying their biggest success in 1969 with the popular single "Bridge Over Troubled Waters." But even in the midst of Simon and Garfunkel's greatest success, Simon was becoming increasingly restless to venture out on his own. "When I'd be sitting off to the side," Simon confessed to an interviewer a few years later, "and Artie [Garfunkel] would be singing 'Bridge,' people would stomp and cheer when it was over, and I would think, 'That's my song, man. Thank you very much, I wrote that song.' "[40]

Art Garfunkel (left) and Paul Simon
perform at a folk concert.

A few years earlier, during the communal spirit of the late
1960s, Simon would probably have been embarrassed to admit his
feelings to the public. By the early 1970s, however, the desire for
individual self-expression and personal recognition had become not
only acceptable but expected from rock and roll's most prominent
personalities.

Among the first rock-and-roll bands to splinter into solo careers for its members was the Beatles. The year 1970 saw the release of Paul McCartney's *McCartney*, George Harrison's *All Things Must Pass*, and John Lennon's *Plastic Ono Band*. The Lennon recording, along with his follow-up release, *Imagine* (1971), was an especially impressive solo performance, featuring his finest work since the Beatles' best recordings during the mid-1960s.

Another important outcome of the folk-rock revival was the opportunity it provided for a number of gifted artists who had previously enjoyed success writing songs for other people during the 1960s to perform their own work for a mass audience. During 1971 and 1972, pop composers such as Randy Newman, Harry Nilsson, Laura Nyro, and Carole King gradually began to inch their way toward the top of the *Billboard* album charts. In the late 1960s, Nilsson and Newman had each composed hit songs for the rock vocal trio Three Dog Night; Nyro had written a number of successful releases for the Fifth Dimension; and King had earned a reputation, along with her husband Gerry Goffin, as one of the best songwriters in the business. Earlier in the decade, the couple had composed a number of pop standards, including Little Eva's "The Locomotion" and the Shirelle's "Will You Still Love Me Tomorrow."

Of all the singer-songwriters to emerge during the period, King enjoyed the greatest success. Encouraged by her friend James Taylor, she released her first solo recording, *Now That Everything's Been Said* in 1968. The album attracted little interest amid the huge assortment of powerful rock-and-roll albums that appeared that year, however. In 1971, King made a second attempt as a solo artist with the release of *Tapestry*. The album was a rich collection of King compositions that blended new, highly personal tunes with her older pop standards. To everyone's surprise, the recording quickly became one of the most successful releases in popular music history. In less than a year, it had sold more than five million copies with its consistently strong tunes and simple, piano-driven arrangements. *Tapestry* appealed to virtually everyone, from rock critics to the young teenage fans who listened to James Taylor. The album would continue to sell in large numbers throughout the 1970s. It remained among *Billboard*'s top 100 albums for an incredible 475 weeks before finally slipping from the charts at the end of the decade.

With *Tapestry* now regarded as one of pop music's most beloved and respected recordings, it seems hard to believe that two of the album's most popular singles were actually censored or withheld from the public during the early 1970s. Many radio stations refused to play "I Feel the Earth Move" and "(You Make Me Feel Like) A Natural Woman" because of the songs' sexually suggestive content. In the past, bands like the Rolling Stones and the Doors had released songs with far more direct and explicit lyrics. King's songs were so controversial—and so important—because they marked the first time on a popular recording that a young woman had sung so openly and so confidently about her own feelings.

The folk-rock and singer-songwriter movements of the early 1970s also inspired the earliest recordings of a number of performers whose music would dominate the charts in the years ahead, including Billy Joel, the Eagles, Fleetwood Mac, Elton John, and Bruce Springsteen. The singer-songwriter tag almost kept two of these artists, Elton John and Bruce Springsteen, from achieving the enormous popularity that they would later achieve throughout the remainder of the decade.

British pianist-composer Elton John—his original name was Reginald Dwight—released his first album, *Empty Sky,* in 1969. The album sold poorly. A second album, *Elton John,* was released the following year and enjoyed somewhat better success, due in large part to the success of the single, "Your Song."

In spite of the commercial disappointment of his early albums, Elton John had gained a wide following on both sides of the Atlantic as a live performer. Sporting huge goggle-like sunglasses and tall stovepipe hats, the short, pudgy singer was a maniac on stage. In his wildly theatrical performances, he kicked his piano stool aside like Jerry Lee Lewis, pranced and howled like Little Richard, and struck flamboyant poses like Liberace in the brightly colored costumes that he often changed between songs. The problem was that his albums, unlike his concerts, were often somber and overproduced. When Elton finally managed to capture the energy and excitement of his live performances on a studio recording, on *Honky Chateau* (1972), his music suddenly began to catch on with the record-buying public. With its hard, staccato, barroom-style piano, *Honky Chateau* quickly rose to number one on the pop charts—a feat that Elton would repeat with his next six albums. During the mid-1970s, he would release some of the era's liveliest and most popular singles, including "Benny and the Jets," "Rocket Man," and "Philadelphia Freedom."

The most significant rock-and-roll performer to emerge from the folk-rock era was Bruce Springsteen. Toward the end of 1972, Columbia Records representative John Hammond was touring the East Coast in search of new talent when he first heard Springsteen and his E Street Band performing at a small New York City club. Hammond, the same brilliant talent scout who had discovered Bob Dylan for Columbia in 1961, was immediately impressed by Springsteen's stage presence and songwriting ability. Columbia quickly signed the young performer and decided, upon Hammond's advice, to bill him to the public as "the new Bob Dylan."

THE SHAGGS

The Shaggs's story began in March 1969, when middle-aged rock enthusiast Austin Wiggins Jr. of Fremont, New Hampshire, decided to produce a recording by his three musically ambitious but completely untrained teenage daughters. Having recently acquired a drum kit and a pair of guitars, the trio had lately been amusing the patrons of local dances and social gatherings with their impromptu onstage rehearsals, and their odd but sweet songs about family values and imaginary pets. There were no conventional chords or melodies in the girls' music, but the songs were somehow held together by the stubborn intensity of the band's weird notes and rhythms and the absolute sincerity of their offbeat lyrics and flat, monotone vocals.

Although the girls could barely play their instruments, the elder Wiggins was eager to get their music to the record-buying public. "I want to capture them while they're hot," he explained at the time. After a local distributor left

Springsteen's first two albums, *Greetings from Asbury Park* and *The Wild, the Innocent and the E Street Shuffle* (both released in 1973), contained a number of spirited numbers, including "Rosalita" and "Blinded by the Light." The emphasis on both recordings, however, was definitely on the performer's rare gifts as a lyricist and the softer, folksier side of his personality. As with Elton town with Wiggins' money and most of the copies of the band's record, Philosophy of the World, the Shaggs seemed destined for obscurity. In the early 1970s, however, a deejay at WCBN-FM, a popular Boston radio station, came across a copy of the record and began to feature it on his broadcasts. Before long, the group had gained the attention and the admiration of listeners like Terry Adams of the band NRBQ and Frank Zappa, who insisted that the band was "better than the Beatles." Philosophy of the World was quickly rereleased by Rounder Records and a second, slightly more polished recording was made in 1975. In 1980, Philosophy received yet another rerelease, earning the band the honor of being named *Rolling Stone*'s Comeback Band of the Year and a lot of rolled eyes from members of the recording community who thought the whole thing was a joke. Twenty-five years and several reissues after their debut recording, the Shaggs remain one of the most unusual and controversial events in the history of rock and roll.

John, Springsteen's earliest recordings failed to capture the power and vitality of his live shows, and both albums sold poorly at first.

In concert, however, Springsteen and his band continued to draw a following. Performing for up to four hours at a time, they seemed determined to play until they collapsed from exhaustion. During a concert, Springsteen would climb on top of a loudspeaker to perform a wrenching guitar solo, slide across the length of the stage on his knees at the end of a chorus, or leap into the middle of the crowd during an instrumental break.

The most exciting moments in Springsteen's shows, however, occurred whenever he and saxophonist Clarence Clemmons faced off together to trade solos at the center of the stage. A huge bear of a man who literally towered above the rest of the band, Clemmons had a deep, powerful tone on saxophone that inspired Springsteen to give his very best performances. For many rock-and-roll fans, the two men's spirited duets on songs like "Rosalita" and "Growing Up" were the purest, most riveting rock and roll since Little Richard his music career for the church in the late 1950s.

Following a Springsteen performance at a small club in Cambridge, Massachusetts, in 1974, *Rolling Stone* critic Jon Landau wrote a review that helped Springsteen finally find a nationwide mainstream audience. "I have seen rock and roll's future," gushed Landau, who would later leave his job as a music journalist to produce Springsteen's recordings, "and his name is Bruce Springsteen."[41]

Suddenly, rock-and-roll fans across the country wanted to know what all the fuss was about. They had their answer the following year, with the release of Springsteen's next album, *Born to Run*. With its explosive rock anthems and Phil Spector–style "wall of sound," the album was one of the most exciting rock-and roll-recordings of the era. Not only did it become a huge commercial success for Columbia Records; Springsteen himself became a nationwide phenomenon. In one week alone, the new rock-and-roll star appeared on the covers of both *Time* and *Newsweek*. It was the most news generated by a rock-and-roll act since the Beatles made their first U.S. appearance in February 1963.

From the beginning, however, Springsteen was a reluctant

Bruce Springsteen belts out his hit song "Born in the U.S.A." before a sell-out crowd as he kicks off his 1985 U.S. tour in Washington, D.C.

superstar. He seemed genuinely to prefer the intimacy of small clubs to the huge concert halls and arenas that his enormous popularity suddenly required. Four years would pass before he released his next album, *Darkness at the Edge of Town* (1979). On *Darkness* and the albums that followed, Springsteen presented a much

103

darker, more brooding picture of life in America than on his previous recordings. In place of the restless, frustrated young misfits who populated his early tunes, Springsteen's later work told stories of sad, often desperate middle-aged workers whose hopes and dreams had been shattered. Even Springsteen's most popular and danceable tune from the 1980s, "Born in the U.S.A.," had its dark side. Politicians of both parties tried to use the single as their theme song during the 1984 presidential campaign. But the song actually told the story of a country that had turned its back on its citizens.

Springsteen's most openly defiant statement came on the solo album *Nebraska*. Accompanied only by an acoustic guitar, he told story after story about murder, death, and disappointment in the American heartland—all sung in a raw, mournful voice. After almost 15 years, Springsteen had finally become the brilliant folk troubadour that he was originally rumored to be. Unfortunately, few people seemed to care, and *Nebraska* became the artist's poorest-selling recording.

During the singer-songwriter era of the early 1970s, a number of folk-rock bands gained widespread popularity among rock music fans. The most notable of these new folk-rock bands were Creedence Clearwater Revival, the Band, and Crosby, Stills, Nash and Young.

The folk-rock movement had actually begun in the mid-1960s when Los Angeles bands—like the Byrds, the Buffalo Springfield, and the Flying Burrito Brothers—began introducing folk and country elements into their spirited performances. Led by singers Roger McGuinn and David Crosby, the Byrds used sweet harmonies and roaring 12-string electric guitars to popularize the songs of folk singers like Pete Seeger ("Turn, Turn, Turn") and Bob Dylan ("Mr. Tambourine Man"). The Buffalo Springfield, and its gifted lead singer-guitarists Stephen Stills and Neil Young, brought elements of

Crosby, Stills, Nash and Young perform in 1969. The members of the band are: (left to right) Neil Young, David Crosby, Graham Nash, and Stephen Stills.

folk, country, and bluegrass music to their lively rock-and-roll tunes, such as "Bluebird," "Rock and Roll Woman," and the classic protest song, "For What It's Worth." Gram Parsons and the Flying Burrito Brothers brought a rougher, more traditional edge to their songs. Parsons, who would also record an album with the Byrds (1968's brilliant *Sweetheart of the Rodeo*), later enjoyed a brief career as a singer-songwriter before his untimely death from a drug overdose in 1973.

In 1969, Stephen Stills, who had recently disbanded the Buffalo Springfield, and David Crosby, who had just been fired from the Byrds, lured tenor vocalist Graham Nash away from the English pop group the Hollies to form a vocal trio. On their debut album, Crosby, Stills and Nash used Stills's sinewy guitar solos and the trio's high, chirpy harmonies to present original compositions like "Marrakesh Express" and "Suite: Judy Blue Eyes."

For the band's live debut at Woodstock, Stills recruited his old bandmate Neil Young to play guitar. Young was also allowed to sing some of his own tunes in the high, nasal voice that he was rarely allowed to use with the Buffalo Springfield. The Canadian composer would leave the band within a couple of years to devote more time to his solo career, but not before Crosby, Stills, Nash and Young had released two highly successful recordings, *Déjà Vu* (1970) and the live album *4-Way Street* (1971).

John Fogerty and the other members of Creedence Clearwater Revival began playing together as teenagers in the early 1960s. In bands with names like the Blue Velvets and the Golliwogs, Fogerty, his brother Tom, Stu Cooke, and Doug Clifford developed a reputation as one of the best cover bands in northern California. In the mid-1960s, they had a minor hit with a remake of Van Morrison's "Brown-Eyed Girl."

By the time the band members signed with Fantasy Records in October 1967, they had changed their name to Creedence Clearwater Revival, and Fogerty's own compositions had become the center of their repertoire. With titles like "Born on the Bayou," "Proud Mary," "Green River," and "Bad Moon Rising," Fogerty's songs described dark, shady characters who lived their lives on the bayou, in the backwoods, and on riverboats. Though he was only in his mid-20s, Fogerty had a voice to match his message. The gifted young white vocalist sounded to many of those who had never seen him perform like a 60-year-old blues or cajun shouter, with a bit of Little Richard thrown in at the end of the verse.

More than anything else, Creedence's music sounded like folk music—hard, jangling, rock-inspired folk music. At a time when most American rock-and-roll bands were using psychedelic effects and long instrumental jams, Fogerty and his band played tight, straightforward rock-and-roll tunes. As unfashionable as the band's music was at the time, Creedence became the only American band during the period to achieve the same blend of critical and commercial success as the Beatles. In the two-year stretch of 1969 and 1970, the band released seven top-10 singles, without ever deviating from their style of simple, straightforward rock and roll. In the early 1970s, Creedence would disband under the pressure of a contract dispute. But their recordings remain as one of rock and roll's purest and most vital contributions to American popular music.

While Creedence Clearwater Revival was basically John Fogerty's band, the Canadian group the Band was a collective ensemble in every sense of the word. All five of the Band's musicians contributed to the songwriting, and—with the exception of organist Garth Hudson—they all took turns singing the lead.

The Band consisted of four Canadians—Hudson, guitarist Robbie Robertson, bass player Rick Danko, and pianist Richard Manuel—and one member from the States, drummer Levon Helm. Helm met his future Band mates in the late 1950s while he was touring Canada with rockabilly singer Ronnie Hawkins. Impressed with the Canadian musicians' knowledge of and commitment to rock and roll, Helm recruited them to help him accompany Hawkins back in the United States. Eventually, the Hawks, as they became known, outgrew Hawkins' music and set out on their own. Bob Dylan heard them playing their rich, rowdy ballads in a Los Angeles bar in the mid-1960s and hired them to play behind him on several of his early electric folk-rock performances. Playing behind Dylan, the group earned a new name, the Band, and the unenviable reputation as the best group in rock and roll without a recording contract.

Finally, in 1968, Capitol Records signed the Band, a deal that would produce five brilliant albums over the next five years. The Band's first two albums, *Music from Big Pink* (1968) and *The Band* (1969), contained some of the era's finest and most unusual singles. Like Creedence Clearwater Revival, the Band wrote songs about simple, offbeat characters from the American heartland. Their best tunes—such as "The Weight," "Up on Cripple Creek," and "The Night They Drove Old Dixie Down"—presented vivid, detailed portraits of their characters' sometimes hopeless struggles to make sense out of their lives. For many fans, these songs captured the struggles and disappointments of their own lives. "We thought that the Band's music was the most natural parallel to our hopes, ambitions and doubts," wrote rock critic Greil Marcus in 1975, "and we were right to think so."[42]

In the early 1970s, the Band went on tour with Bob Dylan once again, splitting their shows between Dylan's work and their own original compositions. In 1972, they summed up the most productive period of their career with the double album *Rock of Ages,* one of the finest live rock-and-roll albums ever recorded. Two years later, the Band released another live album, *Before the Flood,* recorded on their tour with Dylan the year before. At the time, rock critic Robert Christgau described the album as "the craziest and strongest rock and roll ever recorded."[43]

The following year saw another joint release by Dylan and the Band. Recorded in 1967, a year before the release of the Band's debut album, *The Basement Tapes* featured previously unreleased original material by both Dylan and the Band, along with the least inhibited performances that either of them would ever put on record.

8
BRING ON THE NOISE

While most of the country was listening to the soft rock of James Taylor, Carole King, and Neil Young, other musicians were taking rock and roll in an entirely different direction. New bands identifying themselves as "hard rock," "heavy metal," "art rock," and "glam rock" became increasingly attractive alternatives for fans who missed the energy, spectacle, and sheer volume of late 1960s rock and roll.

The loudest and most influential of the new hard rock bands was England's Led Zeppelin. Fronted by squealing tenor vocalist Robert Plant and guitar virtuoso Jimmy Page, the band borrowed its best lyrics from old blues songs. Unlike earlier blues-inspired rock-and-roll acts, like Cream, Hendrix, and the Rolling Stones, however, Led Zeppelin were much less conscientious about crediting the blues musicians whose words, tunes, and instrumental techniques they borrowed. But it hardly seemed to matter, since the band's music was so loud and so explosive that the original melodies were almost completely lost beneath the huge instrumental roar—along with the subtlety and complexity of the original lyrics. Whatever blues purists thought about Led Zeppelin's music, many young rock and roll fans loved it. By 1970, the band had quickly released three highly successful albums, becoming the first musical group in almost a decade to replace the Beatles as the most popular band in England's Top of the Pops.

Led Zeppelin became even more popular the following year, with the release of its fourth album, simply titled *Led Zeppelin IV*. Renamed *Zoso* by the band's fans, the recording featured the eight-minute song "Stairway to Heaven." Part acoustic ballad, part heavy metal anthem, the song featured mystical lyrics about May queens and magic spells that captured the imaginations of teenage listeners everywhere. "Stairway to Heaven" would eventually become the most popular song in the history of FM radio, and *Zoso* remains hard rock and heavy metal's most influential recording.

Led Zeppelin's popularity continued throughout the remainder of the decade, in spite of the release of more sophisticated and challenging recordings, such as *Houses of the Holy* (1973). Their enormous success during the period would inspire an entire generation of hard rock and heavy metal bands—from contemporaries, such as Black Sabbath, Blue Öyster Cult, and Aerosmith, to more recent bands like AC/DC, Guns 'n' Roses, and Metallica.

Eventually, rock and roll was bound to attract musicians with backgrounds or interests in classical music, jazz, and other "more serious" types of musical expression. From the late 1960s onward, a number of bands—such as Yes, King Crimson, Genesis, Jethro Tull, and Emerson, Lake and Palmer—began appearing under the banner of "art rock."

The first and most influential of the art rock bands was England's Pink Floyd. Formed in London in the mid-1960s, Pink Floyd was originally a cover band that gained its reputation by playing offbeat versions of familiar blues and rhythm-and-blues tunes. Things got really weird, however, when a young Cambridge art student named Syd Barrett joined the band in 1966.

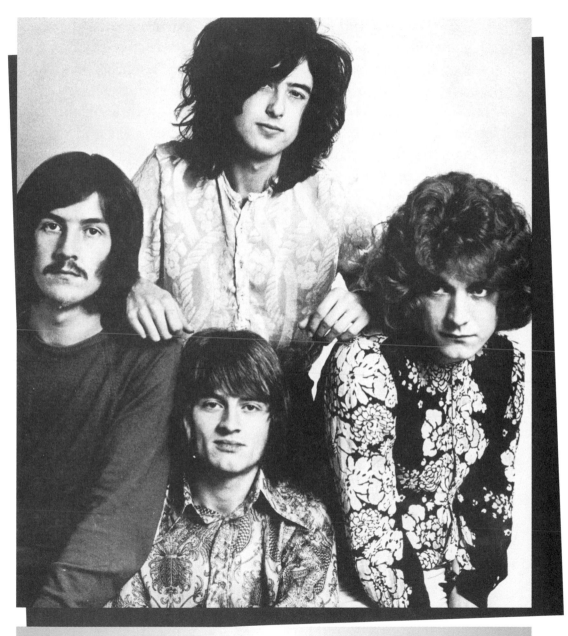

Led Zeppelin, one of the biggest rock supergroups of the 1970s, pose for this publicity shot. The members of the band are (clockwise from top): guitarist Jimmy Page, vocalist Robert Plant, bassist John Paul Jones, and drummer John Bonham.

One of rock and roll's true originals, Barrett shared the other band members' passion for the blues. He even gave the band its name, which he borrowed from two obscure Georgia blues musicians, Pink Anderson and Floyd Council. Like everything else in his life, however, Barrett's version of the blues was a little bit different from everyone else's. While bass player Roger Waters and the rest of the band churned out vaguely recognizable covers of old blues tunes onstage, Barrett used his overly amplified electric guitar to produce an endless array of roaring feedback and strange electronic effects. With Barrett now in control of the band, Pink Floyd's new experimental sound rapidly became the sound track for the London underground art scene.

Syd Barrett was a deeply disturbed young man, however. Even before he joined the band, he had experienced periods of depression and emotional instability. Now, amid the pressures and responsibilities brought on by the band's sudden success, he slowly began to break down. In 1967, Capitol Records released Pink Floyd's debut recording, *Piper at the Gates of Dawn*. A brilliantly unconventional recording for the time, it consisted primarily of Barrett's original compositions, including the wild, drug-inspired instrumental "Interstellar Overdrive."

On the verge of a breakdown by the time *Piper at the Gates of Dawn* was released, Barrett at first refused to tour to promote the album. Under pressure from the other band members, he finally agreed to travel to the United States for a series of highly publicized concerts. But he seemed determined to see the group fail. On a televised performance on Dick Clark's *American Bandstand*, Barrett refused to lip-synch the words to the song "See Emily Play." As the cameras began to roll, band mate Roger Waters pretended that he was the song's lead vocalist.

By the time the U.S. tour was completed, Pink Floyd was in

shambles, and the other band members decided that they had endured enough of their lead singer's unpredictable behavior. Barrett was fired from the band and replaced by singer-guitarist David Gilmour, with Roger Waters taking on most of the group's songwriting duties.

Pink Floyd not only survived Barrett's departure, they actually became even more successful in the years that followed. The band's 1973 release, *Dark Side of the Moon*, was the first record to introduce electronic experimental music to a mass audience. The album became one of the most popular recordings of all time, eventually breaking the mark set by Carol King's *Tapestry* for most consecutive weeks on *Billboard*'s top 100.

What Pink Floyd had lost with Barrett's departure, however, was the playfulness and humor that had made even the composer's most experimental music so much fun. Unlike Barrett's whimsical style of art rock, the music of the later Pink Floyd was much more somber and self-important. For better or worse, Pink Floyd's seriousness would set the tone for many of the other art-rock bands to follow.

The most talented and innovative of the new art-rock bands was England's King Crimson. Formed in 1969 by the brilliant guitarist Robert Fripp, the band released several influential albums during its brief five-year existence. The only problem was that Fripp never really considered himself to be a rock-and-roll performer. In fact, he genuinely deplored the spontaneity and onstage theatrics that characterized most rock-and-roll acts. Instead, Fripp sat calmly on a stool during the band's concerts, playing his wildly innovative guitar licks as if he were sitting in the studio.

King Crimson's most loyal fans found Fripp's cool, controlled performances appealing, but King Crimson's restrained performance style did little to gain the band a mass audience among teenage listeners. During the early 1970s, King Crimson featured some of England's most talented rock-and-rock musicians, but few of them stayed around for long. On the band's five recordings during the period, Fripp never managed to record twice with the same lineup of musicians.

In 1974, King Crimson finally dissolved, with Fripp taking his compositions and guitar techniques in a more experimental, less rock-oriented direction. During the next two decades, he would occasionally bring some of the band's original musicians back together for a new King Crimson album and tour. But it was the band's brief but explosive period of creativity during the early 1970s that made the most lasting contribution to rock and roll.

In contrast to King Crimson's detached performance style, other British artists during the period were busy seeing just how far they could push the wild, theatrical side of rock and roll. The originators of glitter rock—or glam rock, as it was often called by fans—could be easily recognized before they played a single note. Their usual outfits consisted of outrageous, brightly colored clothes, high platform shoes, and lots and lots of makeup. The best glam rock songs were a hard, throbbing blend of hard rock rhythms and art rock instrumental effects. The music, however, was almost always less important than the image. Glam rock portrayed a world in which the misfit had suddenly taken over center stage to become the hero. The use of makeup and extravagant clothes caused some people to wonder about the sexual orientation of glam rockers—and a few of them were either gay or bisexual. But glam rock's appeal extended far beyond the gay community; its music and style were meaningful for all types of young people who had been misunderstood or made fun of by other teenagers.

The first two glam rockers to make a name for themselves in England were Marc Bolan and Gary Glitter. With his round, chubby frame stuffed into a gold glitter-coated jumpsuit, Glitter wobbled around the stage in his high-heeled boots like an aging Las Vegas crooner. But he sang with such enthusiasm and intensity that he quickly became one of glam rock's most popular performers—at least in England. Audiences in the United States were less impressed with Glitter's awkward stage presence. Although his singles typically rose to the top of the British charts, he enjoyed only one hit single in the United States, the hard-rocking anthem "Rock and Roll (Part 2)."

In contrast to Glitter, Marc Bolan took himself and his music very seriously. Bolan (his original name was Mark Feld) started his career in the late 1960s as an offbeat folk singer in the mold of Syd Barrett. In his early band, Tyrannosaurus Rex, Bolan and his partner, Steve Peregrine Took, sang sweet, wistful ballads about wood nymphs, leprechauns, and the haunting British countryside. After Took left the group in 1970, Bolan shortened the band's name to T. Rex and plugged in his guitar. Over the next three years, Bolan and T. Rex produced some of the more memorable rock anthems of the decade, including "Bang a Gong" and "Hot Love." Both glam rock and T. Rex had faded from view by the time Bolan was killed in an automobile accident in September 1975. But the image of Bolan playing his guitar onstage—with his broad bell-bottom jeans, his high platform shoes, and his long, curly hair nearly hidden beneath a tall stovepipe hat—remains one of the more enduring symbols of rock music in the early 1970s.

The most popular of the British glam rockers—and the only one to survive the decline of glam rock in the mid-1970s—was David Bowie. Born David Jones in 1947, Bowie, like Bolan, also began his career as a folk singer during the late 1960s. But Bowie's eccentric appearance and harsh vocal delivery were ill-suited for a folk-rock audience, and he soon shifted his attention to a louder and more theatrical style of performance.

Bowie first flirted with glam rock stardom with the release of

Hunky Dory (1972), a smart, imaginative mix of the singer's early psychedelic folk music with powerful rock anthems like "Queen Bitch." Amid various references to cross-dressing, space aliens, and religious imagery, Bowie described a world in which the unconventional, outrageous behavior of the younger generation was literally driving its "mamas and papas insane" (as he sang in "Oh! You Pretty Things"). But Bowie was generous enough to make room even for some parents in his ideal world. On "Kooks," he sang a lullaby about a glam-rock couple determined to raise their children to be just as odd and uncompromising as they are.

It was Bowie's next release, however, *The Rise and Fall of Ziggy Stardust and the Spiders from Mars* (1972), that really made him an international star. The entire recording told the story of Ziggy, a brilliantly gifted but sadly misunderstood rock star from

David Bowie performs as Ziggy Stardust in 1971. Bowie was the leading figure in the glam-rock scene of the early 1970s.

outer space. A thinly veiled tribute to the late Jimi Hendrix, the album featured inspired performances by Bowie and guitarist Mick Ronson on some of the hardest, most aggressive rock and roll that had ever graced a commercially successful recording. For the entire time that Bowie and his band toured to promote the album, he retained the costume and the character of Ziggy Stardust—both in and out of concert. With his spiked hair dyed carrot red, his thick stage makeup, and his high-tech wardrobe, Bowie/Ziggy quickly became rock and roll's most controversial and popular live performer.

In addition to individual stars like Bolan, Glitter, and Bowie, English glam rock also inspired a number of important bands, including Mott the Hoople and Roxy Music. Mott the Hoople and their growling lead vocalist, Ian Hunter, had already put out a couple of albums before they caught David Bowie's attention in 1972. Bowie was so impressed with the band's outrageous stage act and Hunter's distinctive blend of glam rock and Bob Dylan–style folk rock that he offered them the chance to be the first to record his new song, "All the Young Dudes." Released toward the end of the year, the song, which was also produced by Bowie, became the anthem for the glam rock movement and propelled Mott the Hoople into stardom both in England and the United States.

Roxy Music had a darker, more sophisticated sound than many of their glam-rock contemporaries. Led by vocalist Bryan Ferry and synthesizer player-producer Brian Eno, the band had the same uneasy mix of melody and experimentation that characterized the best work of the Beatles and Pink Floyd. Eno was as impatient with the rock-and-roll format as his friend and future collaborator Robert Fripp. He left the band in 1973 before the release of their masterpiece, *Stranded*. With Ferry's brooding, sometimes melodramatic vocals, Phil Manzanera's haunting guitar, and the classic single "Mother of Pearl," the album may be glam rock's finest musical statement. With Eno out of the picture, the band released a string of less experimental and more commercially successful albums throughout the remainder of the decade and into the 1980s, including the darkly romantic *Avalon* (1982).

Closely related to art rock and glam rock was the attempt by several bands during the period to combine the best elements of jazz and rock and roll in their music. Probably the single most influential jazz recording for many rock-and-roll musicians was saxophonist John Coltrane's 1964 masterpiece, *A Love Supreme*. Coltrane's dark, swirling solos inspired countless rock-and-roll guitarists, including Jimi Hendrix, Jerry Garcia, Carlos Santana, and John McLaughlin. In 1967, Irish songwriter Van Morrison borrowed members of the great jazz bassist Charles Mingus's ensemble for his breakthrough release, *Astral Weeks*. Throughout the next two decades, Morrison would continue to include jazz in both his live performances and recordings, such as *Moondance* (1970) and *Wavelength* (1978).

Although his background was in the blues, Traffic's Steve Winwood brought a tense, jazzy feel to the British band's best recordings. On their early albums, Winwood combined his loose, improvisational piano style with guitarist Dave Mason's tight, cheerful pop melodies to produce rock classics, such as "Feelin' All Right" and "Dear Mr. Fantasy." On the band's later releases, like *John Barleycorn Must Die* (1970) and *The Low Spark of High-heeled Boys* (1971), Winwood gave much freer reign to his spacious, jazz-oriented approach to rock-and-roll performance and composition.

Perhaps the most successful fusion of rock and roll and jazz in a popular recording was Blood, Sweat and Tear's 1967 classic *The Child Is Father to the Man*. Band leader Al Kooper had already made a name for himself in his blues-rock band, the Blues Project, and as organist on Dylan's early electric recordings. On the first Blood, Sweat and Tears album, he successfully combined elements of rock, pop, jazz, and the blues to fashion a musical statement that sounds as fresh and unique today as it did when it was first released. Sadly, Kooper left the band shortly after its first album was completed. With his replacement, David Clayton Thomas, singing lead, Blood, Sweat and Tears remained a gifted pop band, but with little of the tension and energy that characterized its first album.

Chicago followed a similar trajectory. The Chicago-based brass-rock ensemble quickly deteriorated during the early 1970s from the loud, guitar-driven jazz-rock collective of its first two recordings, *Chicago Transit Authority* and *Chicago*, into a rather bland and predictable pop group.

9
ROCK GOES UNDERGROUND

While glam rock was conquering England during the early 1970s, a small, defiant group of American musicians were creating their own unique style of misfit rock and roll. Groups like Kiss, Alice Cooper, Iggy and the Stooges, and the New York Dolls resembled British glam rockers in their use of makeup, odd costumes, and outrageous stage shows. The American groups presented a gloomy, grittier image, however, and played a harsher, uglier style of rock and roll than their English contemporaries.

The unofficial leader of this uniquely American version of glam rock was New Yorker Lou Reed. Despite his rough exterior, Reed was an extremely literate young man when he formed the Velvet Underground in New York in the mid-1960s. Earlier in the decade, he had studied writing with the brilliantly gifted but emotionally disturbed poet Delmore Schwartz. The encounter with Schwartz would deeply influence both the pessimism and the sad beauty of Reed's best song lyrics for the band.

When pop artist Andy Warhol first heard the Velvet Underground in 1966, Reed and his main collaborator in the band, John Cale, were already experimenting with the same mix of melody and feedback that Syd Barrett was using in England. They divided their songs between dark, desperate songs about violence and drug addiction ("Heroin," "I'm Waiting for the Man," and "The Gift") and lovely, tender ballads like "Pale Blue Eyes" and "Stephanie Says." With Warhol behind them, the band members quickly became the darlings of the late-1960s art scene and a favorite of music critics. The Velvet Underground never found a wider audience, however, and the band's remarkable albums and singles rarely found their way onto the charts.

Cale left the Velvet Underground in 1968, and the band broke up for good two years later. At the time, Reed seemed genuinely confused about his future. Should he now become a more mainstream artist or continue with the odd experimental music he had been pursuing with his old band? After a failed attempt at glam rock stardom on *Transformer* (1972), Reed began pursuing a darker, harsher, and more personal vision of glam rock. With the exception of the spirited live album, *Rock 'n' Roll Animal* (1974), he seemed determined to alienate even his most loyal fans, taking his music into new and less popular directions with each new release. Reed's most outrageous musical statement appeared on *Metal Machine Music* (1975). With no melodies, no rhythms, and not an instrument in sight, the recording was one loud, continuous burst of controlled electronic feedback. Even at his most unorthodox, however, there were people who were listening carefully to Reed's music. His hard, stripped-down, intensely personal version of rock and roll would have a tremendous impact on many of the punk and new wave bands of the late 1970s.

Alice Cooper and Kiss took things a little less seriously. Detroit-based Alice Cooper's alter ego, Vincent Furnier, delighted and sometimes terrified teenage fans by taking the stage dressed as a ghoulish, blood-stained character straight out of a second-rate

121

horror film. "Sometimes half the audience would be up and out before we finished our first number," he later bragged to an interviewer. "A lot of them, though, were afraid to walk out. They were afraid to move."[44] The band's hard, aggressive anthems, such as "18" and "School's Out," celebrated teenage life and the open defiance of adult authority.

New Yorkers Gene Simmons and Paul Stanley used simpler, more formulaic rock tunes and a more cartoonish, less-threatening stage presence to turn Kiss into one of the nation's most popular live acts during the mid-1970s. The band crashed onto the stage as part devils, part clowns, and part space aliens in their heavy stage makeup and bright, futuristic costumes.

Iggy Pop and the New York Dolls shocked their audiences simply by the way they sounded and behaved on stage. Born James Osterberg, Iggy Pop—or Iggy Stooge as he was sometimes called—was an unusual performer even by the rough, hard-rocking standards of the Detroit underground. Onstage, Iggy would flail his skinny arms, burst into a wild, spastic dance, and then jump into the middle of the crowd—whatever it took to express his own frustration. At a time when hard rock had grown increasingly stagy and theatrical, Iggy and his band communicated absolute sincerity to their audience, and the Stooges and their harsh, ugly music gained a small but loyal group of followers.

The New York Dolls brought the same level of outrageous enthusiasm to the stages of Max's Kansas City and the other dark, smoke-filled New York clubs where they first appeared during the early 1970s. The first thing one noticed about the Dolls was how horrible they sounded. Though they looked the part of glam rockers—with their white pancake makeup, bright clothes, and high platform shoes—none of the band members knew how to play their instruments. Completely unfazed by their own lack of skill, gravel-

Iggy Pop is pumped up and ready to rock all night.

throated vocalist David Johansen, guitarist Johnny Thunders, and the other band members plowed through their early performances like a drunken, revved-up version of the Rolling Stones. Their albums, *New York Dolls* (1973) and *Too Much Too Soon* (1974), managed to communicate much of the wild, reckless energy of their early live shows.

"I couldn't believe how anybody could be so bad," Malcolm McLaren, who would later manage the Sex Pistols, said of his first encounter with the Dolls. "I was suddenly impressed that I was no longer concerned with whether you could play well. Whether you were able to even know about rock 'n' roll to the extent that you were able to write songs properly wasn't important any longer. The Dolls impressed upon me that there was something else. There was something wonderful. I thought how brilliant they were to be this bad."[45]

During this same period, a new wave of African-American musicians like James Brown, Sly Stone, Curtis Mayfield, Isaac Hayes, and George Clinton were developing their own musical vision of urban life. For all its strengths, the music of Motown had begun to seem much too cheerful and optimistic for many young black listeners.

One of the most innovative and optimistic singer-composers of the late 1960s was the former disc jockey, Sylvester Stewart. With his large interracial ensemble, Sly and the Family Stone, Stewart released a string of hit singles during the period that were equally successful with white and black listeners, including "Everyday People," "Stand," and "Everybody Is a Star." As the new decade began, however, Stewart began to lose his sense of optimism along with much of the rest of the nation. Only a year after the phenomenal success of the band's cheerful *Greatest Hits* album, Sly and the Family Stone released the dark, controversial *There's a Riot Goin' On* (1971). In the place of the band's hopeful anthems of the past, the new recording featured bitter, cynical tunes like "A Family Affair" and "Don't Call Me Nigger, Whitey (Don't Call Me Whitey, Nigger)."

The great rhythm-and-blues singer James Brown was another black performer who changed his tune in response to the tensions and conflicts gripping the African-American community. A native of Macon, Georgia, home of Little Richard and Otis Redding, Brown fired his legendary rhythm-and-blues band, the Famous Flames, in 1970 and replaced it with a lighter, louder, and funkier band that included the remarkable young bass player Bootsy Collins. The result not only revitalized Brown's career; it helped to establish "funk" as the dominant force in African-American music during the decade. On singles like "Get Up, I Feel Like Being a Sex Machine" and "Say It Loud (I'm Black and I'm Proud)," Brown's jerky, percussive new music perfectly captured the mood of black urban life in the early 1970s.

The most significant figure in the funk movement, however, was composer-band leader George Clinton. Born in 1940, Clinton formed a rhythm-and-blues vocal group called Parliament as a teenager in New Jersey during the mid-1950s. He managed to keep the group together long enough to earn its only top 20 hit with 1967's "(I Just Wanna) Testify." By the time "Testify" reached the charts, however, Clinton had moved on to a different kind of music. Inspired by the harsh, propulsive rhythms of James Brown and the heroic guitar techniques of Jimi Hendrix, he left Parliament shortly after "Testify" was released and moved to Detroit. In Detroit, Clinton became part of the same underground culture that produced Alice Cooper, the Stooges, and the hard psychedelic blues band the MC-5. Clinton absorbed it all, soon developing his own style of theatrical, guitar-driven funk.

"Funk was the future," he later told an interviewer, "but it started to catch on because it was a total rejection of the smooth and slick Motown-type of sound. Black people had become fed up with the dress-alike, dance-routine type of music."[46]

Clinton's first funk band, Funkadelic, was a 12-piece orchestra that combined outlandish, often obscene lyrics, hard funk rhythms, huge guitar solos, and an elaborately theatrical performance style. The band's best singles, such as "Maggot Brain" and "Tear the Roof Off the Sucker (Give Up the Funk)," became anthems for the nation's underground black youth culture.

As Clinton's success increased among black audiences, his stage shows became bigger and more elaborate. They eventually rivaled the spectacles created by Bowie, Elton John, Kiss, and Pink

Floyd during the mid-1970s. As his stage show grew, so did his roster of talented young musicians. In 1974, he added another large ensemble, called Parliament, to his touring and recording company. Over the years, Clinton's Parliament-Funkadelic All-Stars have included such funk and rhythm-and-blues standouts as Bootsy Collins and keyboardist Bernie Worrell.

During the mid-1970s, however, most Americans—both black and white—were not interested in the harsh, complex music being made by musicians like George Clinton and Sly Stone, or the darker, more primitive visions of Lou Reed, Iggy Pop, and the New York Dolls. Increasingly during the period, young people simply wanted music that would allow them to dance. In 1974, artists like the Hues Corporation, Van McCoy, and KC and the Sunshine Band began releasing light, cheerful dance tunes that combined simple lyrics, Latin rhythms, swirling synthesizers, and just enough funk-style beat to keep things moving. Much of the early disco releases featured slick, flavorless arrangements that could qualify neither as rock and roll nor rhythm and blues. Whatever they were, however, most of the songs were fun to dance to. Suddenly, clubs began opening their doors to groups of people who had not felt welcome as a part of the music scene in more than a decade—young women, gay men and lesbians, and older music fans who no longer found hard, aggressive rock and roll appealing. Most significantly, disco did what neither funk before it nor punk after it could achieve. In cities and towns across the country, it brought young white and black music fans together on the same dance floor.

Disco reached its peak in 1977 with the release of the movie *Saturday Night Fever*, starring John Travolta, and the sound track that accompanied it. The album became the year's most popular recording and one of the biggest-selling albums of all time. The album also turned the English vocal trio the Bee Gees into one of the most popular groups in the world. The band's singles from the

The Bee Gees—(left to right) brothers Robin, Barry, and Maurice Gibb—proudly display their Grammy award for Album of the Year in 1979, which they won for their soundtrack for the film *Saturday Night Fever*.

album, "Stayin' Alive" and "How Deep Is Your Love," hovered near the top of the charts for most of the year.

During the late 1970s, disco produced the novelty dance band the Village People, an openly gay vocal quintet with costumes straight out of a Parliament performance. The band's tongue-in-cheek renditions of "In the Navy," "Macho Man," and "Y.M.C.A." were among the period's biggest hits.

Disco's most important contribution to popular music was pop diva Donna Summer. In a short time, Summer graduated from the whispered moaning of 1975's "Love to Love You, Baby" to her powerful, self-assured performance as a rhythm-and-blues vocalist on 1979's "Bad Girls."

10
ROCK AND ROLL'S LAST STAND

At the height of disco's popularity in the U.S., a radically different style of music was beginning to gain a large following in England. Elements of punk rock, as it would soon be known, had already been heard in the U.S. in the music of Iggy Pop, the New York Dolls, and such mid-1970s artists as Jonathan Richman, Pere Ubu, Patti Smith, and Richard Hell and the Voidoids. It was only after London boutique owner Malcolm McLaren brought together the Sex Pistols in 1976, however, that punk and its do-it-yourself approach to rock and roll really began to attract attention.

In the back rooms of Sex, his fashionable Kings Road boutique, McLaren created the ragged, makeshift wardrobes that would clothe the punk movement during the late 1970s. The window displays at his store featured mannequins with ragged jeans, torn stockings, spiked hair, black leather jackets, and T-shirts spray-painted with angry anarchist slogans like "no future" and "we hate everything." It was all a young person needed to shock and horrify the British establishment. And shock, more than anything else, was at the heart of the punk movement. Poor and uneducated, many young Brits were determined to throw their boredom, frustration, and anger back in the face of the ruling class—in the most shocking way possible. The punk movement, with its angry slogans and violent-looking apparel, was just what these young people needed to get their angry message across to the public.

In addition to the fashion, McLaren wanted to give the punk movement its own unique sound. A decade earlier, Andy Warhol had introduced the New York art scene to its favorite band, the Velvet Underground, and McLaren was determined to play the same role for the London youth movement. In the summer of 1975, McLaren auditioned four London street kids—Steve Jones, Paul Cook, Glen Matlock, and John Lydon—for a new band that he intended to manage. When the foursome began appearing in London clubs as the Sex Pistols a few months later, they were still learning to play their instruments and their songs onstage. But McLaren had clothed his young group in the finest and most frightening anarchist apparel, and equipped them with a sound system powerful enough to rattle the brick walls of the tiny London clubs where they played.

As untrained and undisciplined as they were, the Sex Pistols quickly began to display flashes of real talent in their performances—along with a reckless energy that few people had ever seen before. The rhythms, even when clumsy, were always fast and furious, and guitarist Steve Jones had a hard, slashing style that made the big guitar solos of most hard-rock and heavy-metal bands seem dull and ponderous. Though the band's lead singer, John Lydon, could barely sing in any conventional sense, he had an awkward, desperate stage presence and snarling, hysterical vocals that could be heard above even the noisiest, most hostile crowds. "We knew he couldn't sing," McLaren would later recall, "that he had no sense of rhythm, but he had this charm of a boy in pain, trying to pretend he's cool. That was the most accessible thing."[47] Lydon soon began calling himself Johnny Rotten, a name that perfectly matched his behavior and appearance both on and off the stage.

In England at least, the Sex Pistols were one of the most spectacular—and briefest—success stories in the history of rock and roll. By the time their debut album, *Never Mind the Bollocks*, began climbing the British charts in 1977, the group had already begun to unravel under the pressure of touring, ongoing contract disputes, and constant battling with the conservative British press. Bassist Glen Matlock was soon replaced by Lydon's childhood

The Sex Pistols—bassist Sid Vicious, drummer Paul Cook, vocalist Johnny Rotten, and guitarist Steve Jones—rip through a song during their disasterous 1978 U.S. tour.

friend John Simon Ritchie, who immediately changed his name to Sid Vicious. He was a troubled, sometimes violent young man with an addiction to heroin and virtually no experience on bass guitar.

By the time the band arrived in the United States for a two-week tour early in 1978, the Sex Pistols had all but disbanded. From the beginning, the American tour was a disaster. *Saturday Night Fever* was the nation's number-one movie at the time, and its disco-oriented sound track was at the top of the album charts. Most American teenagers were much more interested in dancing to the music of the Bee Gees and Donna Summer than in being insulted by a tired, disgruntled group of British punks. Angry and humiliated by the band's failure in the United States, Lydon left the Sex Pistols shortly after their final U.S. show at the Winterland concert hall in San Francisco. Lydon would resurface a few months later with a new band, Public Image Ltd. (PiL), and the same defiant, uncompromising attitude. By the end of the year, Sid Vicious would be dead of an apparent heroin overdose. At the time of his death, Vicious was awaiting trial for the murder of his girlfriend Nancy Spungen.

Even before the Sex Pistols broke up, a new London musical foursome had begun to challenge the band's position as the premier British punk band. The members of the Clash were every bit as angry and defiant as the Sex Pistols, but with an outspoken political commitment that gave young people a place to direct their frustration and disappointment. Led by guitarists Joe Strummer and Mick Jones, the Clash were also one of the finest rock-and-roll bands ever to commandeer a stage.

"The Clash," remembered Steve Connolly, one of the group's earliest fans, "were the first band to steal fans from the Pistols: they were the construction to the Sex Pistols' nihilism. The two go hand in hand to a certain extent, and John [Lydon] and the Pistols decried the fact, but . . . you couldn't just lay your head against the wall."[48]

A former rockabilly musician, Strummer formed the band after watching an early Sex Pistols show in 1976. The snarling, often explosive Strummer and the quieter, more thoughtful Jones quickly became the Lennon-McCartney of the punk movement, writing fast, abrasive anthems about poverty, racism, and social injustice. The band's commitment to social protest was strongly influenced by their exposure to London's militant Rastafarian community. Founded by African-American leader Marcus Garvey in the 1920s, the Rastafarian tradition was a powerful symbol of protest and hope for the oppressed people of Jamaica, many of whom were living in England at the time. In addition to their outspoken political beliefs, the Rastafarians also had a very distinctive style of music, called reggae. From their earliest performances, the Clash were heavily influenced by the great reggae poet Bob Marley and his band, the Wailers. Reggae's lazy, half-spoken vocals and tumbling, broken rhythms became an important part of the Clash's music.

Unlike the Sex Pistols, the Clash would stay together for several years before Strummer and Jones split to form their own bands in the early 1980s. The Clash's first three albums for CBS Records—*The Clash* (1977), *Give 'Em Enough Rope* (1978), and *London Calling* (1979)—are probably the finest recordings to emerge from the punk era. They are also among the best rock-and-roll recordings ever made.

Inspired by the success of the English punk movement, a new group of punk-style bands in New York City had begun to cause a stir at downtown venues like the Mud Club and CBGB. Each night, young fans, decked out in spiked hair, ripped jeans, and combat boots, stood in line to hear bands like DNA, Television, Richard Hell and the Voidoids, and Teenage Jesus and the Jerks.

The most successful of the bands to make their names at CBGB were the Ramones, Blondie, and the Talking Heads. The local punk quintet the Ramones may have sounded like they were playing the same song over and over again, but people loved their wild, energetic music, black leather jackets, Beatles-style bangs, and self-deprecating humor. Their songwriting formula generally included a sweet, catchy melody sung over a simple three-chord progression played as loud and as fast as was humanly possible. Rarely lasting more than two minutes, songs like "Sheena Is a Punk Rocker" and "I Wanna Be Sedated" were favorites among their energetic, pogo-dancing fans.

Led by singer Deborah Harry, Blondie combined Warhol-style glam-rock indifference, breathy girl-group vocals, and a tight punk rhythm section. Harry's icy good looks and ease in handling the pressures of the media helped make the band the first national celebrities of the New York punk movement. Equal parts glossy pop and hard-edged punk, the band's breakthrough album, *Parallel Lines*, was as close as punk would ever come to mainstream acceptability.

The best of the New York punk bands was the Talking Heads. Fronted by lead singer-composer David Byrne, the Talking Heads made it acceptable for punk bands to be smart, both musically and otherwise. Byrne sang in a clipped, high-pitched whine that sounded sometimes like an urgent gospel shouter and sometimes like a deranged robot, with an occasional Buddy Holly–style hiccup thrown in at the end. The band had already made three strong recordings by the time they released their masterpiece, *Remain in Light* (1980). Produced by Brian Eno, the album was one of the few recordings from the period to successfully combine the intensity of punk with the rhythmic complexity of black musicians like George Clinton and James Brown.

Back in England, a "new wave" of punk-influenced bands had begun to gain attention. Some of the more important British bands of the late 1970s included the Fall, the Jam, the Mekons, and the Police. The phenomenal success of the latter band later launched the career of its lead singer, Sting. During the 1980s, he would become one of the most popular singers in both England and the United States.

No British act gained more attention during the period, however, than singer-songwriter Elvis Costello. Born Declan McManus, the lanky, bespectacled singer resembled a punk-rock version of Buddy Holly. In concert, he learned so far into the microphone during the verses that it seemed he might fall on his face, then stumbled quickly back to attack his guitar.

Unlike other punk albums of the day, the instrumentals on Costello's debut recording, *My Aim Is True*, were clean and crisp enough to bring his angry vocals clearly to the front. The words, after all, were what made Costello's music so special. Like Dylan in the early 1960s, clever, imaginative lyrics seemed to pour naturally from the singer's mouth. In the four-year period between 1977 and 1980, he released four remarkable albums and a body of songs that placed him in the elite ranks of rock-and-roll composers. Some of his biggest hits from the period included "Allison," "Watching the Detectives," and "The Angels Want to Wear My Red Shoes." If the Talking Heads made it acceptable for a punk rocker to be smart, Costello made it okay to be brilliant. His best music during the late 1970s and early 1980s expanded punk rock's audience to include many people who might have never otherwise given it a chance.

11
IT'S ALL IN THE IMAGE

By almost any standard, the 1980s were a disappointing period for rock and roll. In the late 1970s, punk bands like the Sex Pistols, the Clash, and the Talking Heads had tried to bring new life to rock music by replacing the slick, formulaic music of disco and arena rock with their own simpler, more aggressive performances.

In the early 1980s, however, a new wave of British and American bands began climbing the charts with a lighter, more accessible version of punk. For many listeners, bands like the Cars, R.E.M., U2, and the Cure were no longer challenging the tastes and values of the music establishment; they *were* the music establishment. Their highly successful recordings and tours proved that even the fury and simplicity of punk rock could be made into a marketable formula.

"Rock 'n' roll," wrote music critic Greil Marcus in 1980, echoing the opinions of his fellow music critic Ed Ward, "which used to be about breaking rules, now seems to be about learning them."[49]

To make matters worse, rock-and-roll fans were shocked on December 8, 1980, by the news that former Beatle John Lennon had been shot to death by a disturbed fan outside his home in the Dakota apartment building in Manhattan. It was hard for many people to disagree with John Lydon's pronouncement at a news conference that "rock and roll is dead." Of course, Lydon's statement was made during the same interview in which he announced that he had just formed a new rock-and-roll band, Public Image Ltd., or PiL. Rock and roll may have died during the late 1970s, but Lydon and a host of other rock and rollers still had a lot invested in its survival.

Following Lydon's example with PiL, a few young U.S. bands began making music that was so loud, so harsh, and so poorly produced that there was little, if any, possibility of mainstream acceptance. Recording for small independent labels like Rough Trade, SST, and TwinTone, these new "alternative" bands produced some of the finest—and least heard—music of the decade. Among the highlights were the Replacements' *Let It Be*, Sonic Youth's *Daydream Nation*, Husker Dü's *Zen Arcade*, and the Minutemen's *Double Nickels on a Dime*. At their best, these new bands combined hard, aggressive rhythms and pure, irresistible melodies as successfully as Little Richard, Jimi Hendrix, and the Clash had done before them. At their worst, they simply made noise.

While Sonic Youth and the Replacements were playing their music for a small, devout following in clubs and small concert halls, the majority of rock-and-roll fans were sitting quietly in front of their television. In 1980, the 24-hour music network MTV began broadcasting music videos by mainstream rock and pop artists on televisions across the United States. Not only did MTV give fans a chance to see their favorite performers on television each day; it also changed the way most people looked at and listened to rock and roll. As MTV became more popular throughout the decade, the way musicians looked and acted on-screen became

ALEX CHILTON

Memphis native Alex Chilton never wanted to be a rock-and-roll star. The leader singer for the late-1960s pop group the Box Tops, the teenage Chilton reportedly filled himself with huge late-night doses of whiskey and cigarettes to make his sweet tenor voice sound tough and husky enough for the chart-topping "Soul Deep," and "Cry Like a Baby." Just as the band's songs were reaching the top of the charts, Chilton quit and disappeared from recording. In the early 1970s, he reappeared to form Big Star with his hometown pal, Chris Bell. Combining the crisp pop melodies of the Beatles and the Beach Boys with the harsh, crunching rhythms of hard rock and heavy metal, Big Star would be imitated by dozens of alternative rock bands over the next 25 years, from R.E.M. to the Replacements. One of the best and most innovative bands of the 1970s, Big Star made three brilliant albums before Chilton grew tired of the musical formula that he had perfected and disappeared from recording once again in the middle of the decade. Since then, the eccentric composer-performer has come out of hiding every couple of years to release a string of always offbeat, occasionally brilliant solo recordings, with songs ranging from Memphis rhythm and blues to sentimental show tunes to hard-rock anthems. To this day, he remains a hero for thousands of musicians and fans for whom deeply personal, uncompromising music—and not fame and money—remain the real promise of rock and roll.

Revelers party at MTV's 1982 New Year's Eve Ball. The advent of music videos profoundly changed the face of rock and roll.

arguably more important than how they sounded on their records. Soon the recordings of groups like Duran Duran and Aha, known more for their good looks than their good music, began to rise to the top of the pop charts.

During the mid-1980s, MTV also helped launch the solo careers of two of the decades most popular and controversial recording artists: Michael Jackson and Madonna.

138

In 1978, 19-year-old Madonna Louise Veronica Ciccone dropped out of the University of Michigan's School of Music to pursue a career as a dancer in New York. After arriving in New York, Madonna quickly became a part of the city's hip art and music scene. She spent much of her time in fashionable dance clubs like Danceteria, Hurrahs, and CBGB in the company of friends like artists Keith Haring and Jean-Michel Basquiat. During this period, Madonna also began to sing. In the same clubs where she once went just to dance, she began performing her own energetic dance tunes using a style that combined disco's light grooves and the tough, street-smart attitude of punk.

A tireless self-promoter, Madonna gained the attention of a Warner Brothers talent scout while she was performing at Danceteria. The label immediately signed her to a contract, and in July 1983, her debut album, simply titled *Madonna*, was released.

Neither the album nor its first single, "Holiday," gained much attention at first. Madonna believed in her recording, however, and she allowed nothing—not even the lackluster promotion by the record label—to discourage her. During the next few months, she promoted her record on her own, singing and dancing in local clubs and discos almost every night.

After "Holiday" reached *Billboard*'s top 100, MTV agreed to screen videos of Madonna's next two singles "Borderline" and "Lucky Star," which would establish the image that would follow Madonna throughout her career—a proud, defiant street kid determined to get what she wants. With the national exposure from MTV, Madonna's records began to climb higher in the charts. By the end of 1983, "Lucky Star" had reached the top 10, an achievement Madonna would repeat with her next 15 singles. Only Elvis Presley had ever put together such an impressive streak of hit records.

The next year, 1984, was the most important of Madonna's career. Her second album, *Like a Virgin*, quickly rose to the top of the charts, along with singles of the title cut and "Material Girl." During the year, Madonna also appeared in her first feature film, costarring with actress Rosanna Arquette in Susan Seidelman's *Desperately Seeking Susan*. Both the movie and Madonna's performance drew rave reviews from the critics.

During the remainder of the decade, Madonna's movie career would falter. Probably the worst experience of her career came in 1986, when she starred along with her husband, Sean Penn, in *Shanghai Surprise*. The film was a complete disaster, both commercially and critically. In addition, rumors of her offscreen quarrels with Penn began to gain more attention in the press than her recordings or performances.

Madonna thrived on controversy, however. In addition to her ongoing quarrels with Penn, whom she divorced in 1989, she shocked the public with her revealing outfits and her controversial opinions on sex and religion. In 1989, she followed the release of

Madonna strikes a demure pose for this publicity shot. The savvy singer has displayed a uncanny knack for remaking her public image, setting styles, and arousing controversy.

140

her most musically accomplished album, *Like a Prayer*, with a video of the title cut that managed to offend just about everyone. The video presented religious images, such as the crucifixion and the Virgin Mary, along with the singer's typically seductive dancing and dress. Many religious groups protested the video, and MTV briefly refused to air it. Madonna, however, claimed that she had made both the song and the video in good faith. She told the press that she had not meant to offend anyone. To prove her point, Madonna dedicated the song and the album, "to my mother, who taught me how to pray."[50] Fueled by the controversy, both the song and the album quickly soared to the top of the charts.

Since *Like a Prayer*, Madonna has been taken more seriously by the mainstream music establishment as both a singer and a songwriter. In his review of the album for *Rolling Stone* music critic J. D. Considine hailed Madonna as "one of the most compelling voices of the eighties."[51]

Even after she had established herself as both a commercially and critically successful artist, Madonna still went out of her way to shock the public. Her 1990 video "Justify My Love" was so sexually explicit that MTV refused to show it. And in her 1991 documentary film, *Truth or Dare*, she offended many viewers with her open discussions of her relationships with her father and her past and present lovers. Predictably both the video and the film were enormously successful.

As Madonna candidly confessed in *Truth or Dare*: "I know I'm not the best singer. I know I'm not the best dancer. But I'm not interested in that. I'm interested in pushing people's buttons."[52]

Pop singer Michael Jackson first gained national recognition singing with his older brothers in the Jackson Five during the early 1970s. In 1969, the Gary, Indiana, band made their nationwide debut on the *Ed Sullivan Show*, amid the same type of fanfare that had previously been reserved for Elvis Presley and the Beatles. Millions of teenage listeners were impressed by the group's tightly choreographed dance routines and Michael's sweet preadolescent voice.

With heavy promotion from the band's label, Motown, the Jackson Five's first single, "I Want You Back," rose quickly to the top of the charts. By early 1970, their second release, the frantic dance tune "ABC," had risen all the way to number one. "ABC" was immediately followed by another number-one hit, the soft ballad "I'll Be There."

By this time, Michael and his brothers had outsold bands like the Beatles and Creedence Clearwater Revival to become the most popular recording group in the nation.

During the 1970s, Michael divided his time between his own recording projects (including the number-one single "Ben"), several tours and recordings with his brothers, and an appearance in the movie, *The Wiz*, as the scarecrow. Set in Harlem and with an African-American cast *The Wiz* was a remake of *The Wizard of Oz* in which Jackson starred with his old friend and mentor Diana Ross, who played Dorothy. Although the film was neither a commercial nor a critical success, it gave audiences their first good look at Jackson's considerable skills as a dancer.

In 1979, Jackson made his first serious attempt at a solo career with the release of the album *Off the Wall*. With spirited singles like "Rock with You" and "Don't Stop Till You Get Enough," the recording was a huge success. By the end of the year, it had sold a remarkable seven million copies.

In response to the recording's success, Jackson also began to exhibit the type of shy, withdrawn behavior that would make him such a mystery to his fans. "I may want to just go walking or sit in a tree," he explained to a reporter from the seclusion of his family home, "but everything we do is on TV or in the newspaper. When you're a performer, people want everything. . . . It can be very scary."[53]

Not even the phenomenal success of *Off the Wall* could prepare Jackson or his fans for what happened next. In October 1982, Jackson released his second solo recording, *Thriller.* The album was produced by Quincy Jones and featured a duet with former Beatle Paul McCartney on "The Girl Is Mine." The album sold well from the start, but things really began to take off in May of the following year when Michael appeared with his brothers on the "Motown 25: Yesterday, Today and Forever" television special. More than 50 million viewers watched in awe as Michael debuted his new music and his new dance, the "moonwalk." Following the television appearance, *Thriller* and its first two singles, "Beat It" and "Billie Jean," began to sell at a remarkable pace. Soon MTV, which had earlier refused to air the video of "Beat It," began to include "Billie Jean" in its lineup. By the end of the year, *Thriller* had outsold the sound track to *Saturday Night Fever* to become the most successful recording of all time. It would continue to remain on the charts throughout the decade, eventually selling more than 40 million copies worldwide.

Three years passed before Jackson released a sequel to his record-breaking album. *Bad* (1987) was another impressive recording of slickly produced ballads and dance tunes. It immediately rose to the top of the album charts. By the time the album was released, however, rumors concerning Jackson's strange behavior off the stage had begun to overshadow the public's response to his music. There were reports that Michael had purchased the bones of the Elephant Man, that his best friend was a pet chimpanzee, and that he slept in a "hyperbaric chamber" to preserve his youth.

Most of the talk concerned Jackson's appearance, which had

changed noticeably in the three years between *Thriller* and *Bad*. After a series of plastic surgery procedures, including the bleaching of his hands and face to conceal a chronic skin condition, Jackson looked more like his idol Diana Ross than the young man who danced the moonwalk in the "Billie Jean" video.

The rumors and controversies hardly seemed to matter to Jackson's fans, however. *Bad* sold almost 20 million copies before it disappeared from the charts. Jackson's worldwide tour at the end of the decade was one of the most highly attended performing events of all time.

Unlike Madonna, Jackson was hurt by some of the news stories, especially those concerning his appearance. He withdrew even further from the public. In 1991, Jackson suffered a stunning blow to his public image when he was accused of fondling a young male fan. The charges against Jackson were soon dropped, and a lawsuit filed by the boy's parents was settled out of court. Jackson's reputation was badly damaged, however, along with the quality of his music. His next album, *Dangerous*, released the following year, replaced the contagious enthusiasm of his earlier recordings with a coldness and bitterness that far fewer listeners could relate to. Though the album sold well by most people's standards—more than five million copies in its first year of release—it was a terrible disappointment compared to *Thriller* and *Bad*.

Apart from Michael Jackson's unprecedented success, African-American music had a number of other rock-related highlights during the 1980s. Among the most impressive and influential performers was the Minneapolis singer-guitarist Prince. On his best recordings, such as *Purple Rain*, Prince combined Jackson's skills as a rhythm-and-blues singer with the wild, big-guitar showmanship of George Clinton's funk ensembles.

Reggae also continued to play an important role in rock during the 1980s. Following the example set by bands like the Clash and the Specials, biracial English bands like General Public, English Beat, and the Fine Young Cannibals successfully combined the best elements of rock and roll and Jamaican music on their recordings.

The biggest impact on African-American music and culture, however, was the emergence of rap music, or hip hop, as a major musical force during the late 1980s. Rap music was inspired by the near-spoken cadences of reggae and the muted rage of 1970s urban street poetry. It combined hard, repetitive rhythms; rhymed, harshly spoken verses; and an innovative style of sampling the recordings of other artists. Rap musicians placed the stereo needle in the groove of a vinyl recording and then spun the disk back and forth on the turntable with their fingertips in order to play back parts of the original recording in a broken, rhythmic style. The rough spoken lyrics and rhythmic sampling gave rap music a unique and powerful sound. The best rap musicians were able to capture the feeling of African-American urban life in the same way that musicians like James Brown, Sly Stone, and George Clinton had done more than a decade earlier.

Following the group Run-DMC's hugely successful duet in the late 1980s with the hard-rock band Aerosmith on "Walk This Way," rap music also began to gain a huge following with young white rock-and-roll fans.

Rap music was responsible for some of the most powerful and innovative musical performances of the late 1980s and early 1990s, including KRS-One's *By Any Means Necessary*, Public Enemy's *It Takes a Nation of Millions,* and Ice Cube's *The Predator*. During the same period, a new wave of rap artists, such as the Digable Planets, P.M. Dawn, and Gang Star's Guru, began to introduce the more gentle melodies of jazz, rhythm and blues, and pop music into the performances.

Public Enemy—(left to right) Flavor Flav, Chuck D, and Terminator X—in a 1987 publicity shot. Rap emerged as a major musical and cultural force in the 1980s.

Another important movement during the late 1980s was "world music." Established artists like David Byrne, Peter Gabriel, and Paul Simon released recordings that combined their own rock styles with elements of Brazilian, African, or Afro-Caribbean music. Simon's *Graceland*, which paired the singer's own lyrics with the rhythms and melodies of South African street music, was among the most highly acclaimed releases of the decade. World music quickly became a phenomenon, and recordings by artists like Milton Nascimento, Ladysmith Black Mambazo, Youssou N'Dour, Black Uhuru, Caetano Veloso, and King Sunny Ade could be found in record stores across the nation.

EPILOGUE
BEYOND NIRVANA

Nirvana exploded onto the music scene with the release of its second album, *Nevermind*, in 1991. Childhood friends from Aberdeen, Washington, guitarist Kurt Cobain and bass player Chris Novoselic had been playing together in noisy hard-core bands since the early 1980s. They eventually settled on the name, Nirvana, and a thrashing but melodic sound that would soon make them famous. By the end of the decade, they had also found a permanent drummer, David Grohl, after going through four separate percussionists in the previous four years.

The band had enjoyed popularity for several years throughout the Northwest, but it was only when MTV began to air the video for the band's single "Smells Like Teen Spirit" in the fall of 1991 that Nirvana really began to gain a huge following.

With Cobain's predictable pattern of soft, restrained verses and anguished, explosive bursts on the chorus, Nirvana's music sounded surprisingly like mid-1970s alternative bands such as Husker Dü and the Replacements. But Nirvana's mix of fury and despair was much more suited to the mood of the early 1990s than the mid-1970s. There was also something special about Cobain's voice. At the same time raspingly hoarse and sweetly plaintive, Cobain's singing communicated both the anger and the fear behind his blank expression. On songs like "Lithium," "Drain You," and "Teen Spirit," the band presented, according to rock critic Gina Arnold, "a pristine picture of a frenzied search for meaning among kids who have been given no tools for contemplation whatever—except, of course, electric guitars."[54]

Nevermind quickly became the biggest-selling record of 1992, with more than six million copies sold worldwide. "Grunge," the new name for Nirvana's harsh, jangling style of music, became a national phenomenon. By the end of the year, the recordings of a number of other Seattle-based grunge bands—such as Pearl Jam, Soundgarden, and Mudhoney—had found their way onto the charts.

A lifelong victim of depression, Cobain was never comfortable with rock-and-roll stardom. For the band's next release, *In Utero* (1993), he composed a dark, unrelentingly pessimistic batch of songs that bewildered many of the band's new fans. On *In Utero*, there were few of the instrumental hooks and friendly melodies that had drawn many listeners to *Nevermind*. To no one's surprise, the recording failed to duplicate the success of its predecessor.

Cobain grew increasingly withdrawn and despondent in the months after the album's release. The following year, after a severe bout of depression, Cobain committed suicide at his home in Washington. The young singer's sudden death stunned his listeners in the same way that Buddy Holly's death had shocked a generation of rock-and-roll fans more than 35 years earlier. In the wake of Cobain's death, another Seattle band, Pearl Jam, became the unofficial leader of the grunge movement.

Fans of Nirvana's Kurt Cobain burn a poster at a vigil in his honor. Cobain died on April 8, 1994, from a self-inflicted gunshot wound.

Probably the most significant musical trend to follow Nirvana was the surprising number of female rock-and-roll performers to attract attention during the period. Throughout the early 1990s, female-led bands like the Breeders, Belly, Throwing Muses, and Bikini Kill began to rival the success of alternative mainstays like Pavement, Beck, and Fugazi. Hole, formed by lead singer Courtney Love, the widow of Kurt Cobain, was one of the best and most controversial of the new bands. Other standouts were Björk, Liz Phair, and P. J. Harvey.

The former lead singer of the Sugarcubes, Icelander Björk used her jazz-inspired squeal to produce two of the most accomplished solo albums of the period, *Debut* and *Post*. For *Exile in Guyville*, Chicago-based rock and roller Liz Phair composed a stunning 14-song response to the Rolling Stones classic *Exile on Main Street*. Phair's album gained attention for both its hard, catchy melodies and the singer's fondness for four-letter words. Best of all the new women rock and rollers was Britain's Polly Jo Harvey. Her third release, *To Send You My Love* (1995), was a

Liz Phair performs in 1995. Phair is one of the many female performers at the forefront of rock and roll in the 1990s.

hard, bluesy, organ-driven masterpiece. Behind Harvey's rough, throaty lead vocals, the album delivered the most riveting rock-and-roll performance since *Nevermind*.

As usual, the recording industry sought to profit from the latest musical trends, and new artists were quickly signed to give the public a more accessible version of both grunge and women's alternative rock. In 1995, singer Alanis Morissette released *Jagged Little Pill*, a friendlier, more cleanly produced version of Phair and Harvey's angry, feminist rock and roll that sold more than six million copies. Hootie and the Blowfish, a talented, good-natured South Carolina foursome who performed a cheerful, watered-down version of Pearl Jam's arena rock, became the most popular band in the world. By the end of the year, the band's debut album, *Cracked Rear View*, had sold more than 12 million copies worldwide.

The biggest news of the year, however, was reserved for the biggest rock-and-roll band of all time. After 25 years, the remaining members of the Beatles staged a brief but highly profitable reunion. Early in 1995, they released a double album full of rare outtakes and new versions of two previously unreleased songs. As if the Beatles reunion had not been strange enough news, the year ended with rumors that, after more than 18 years, John Lydon was planning to reunite the Sex Pistols for a tour in the summer of 1996. More than 40 years after it first exploded on the music scene, rock and roll was still full of surprises.

SOURCE NOTES

Introduction

1. Ed Ward, Geoffrey Stokes, and Ken Tucker, *Rock of Ages: The Rolling Stone History of Rock & Roll* (New York: Rolling Stone Press, 1986), p. 106.

Chapter 1

2. Peter Guralnick, *Last Train to Memphis* (Boston: Back Bay/Little, Brown, 1994), p. 96.
3. Ibid., p. 23.
4. Ibid. p. 95.
5. Ward, Stokes, and Tucker, p. 121.
6. Guralnick, p. 437.
7. Lester Bangs, *Psychotic Reactions and Carburetor Dung* (New York: Vintage Books, 1988), p. 216.

Chapter Two

8. *The Rolling Stone Interviews* (New York: Paperback Library, 1971), p. 367.

9. Charles White, *The Life and Times of Little Richard* (New York: Pocket Books, 1985), p. 57.
10. Ward, Stokes, and Tucker, p. 103.
11. White, pp. 91–92
12. Greil Marcus, *Mystery Train: Images of America in Rock 'n' Roll Music* (New York: Plume Books, 1975), p. 264.
13. Ward, Stokes, and Tucker, p. 178.
14. Ibid.
15. *The Rolling Stone Interviews*, p. 178.

Chapter Three

16. Marcus, p. 262.
17. Ward, Stokes, and Tucker, *Rock of Ages*, p. 108.
18. Ibid., p. 115.
19. Ibid., p. 195.
20. Ibid., p. 166.
21. Ibid., p. 166.

Chapter 4

22. Geoffrey Guliano, ed., *The Lost Beatles Interviews* (New York: Plume Books, 1996), p. 5.
23. *The Rolling Stone Interviews*, p. 199.
24. Guliano, p. 69.
25. Ibid.

Chapter 5

26. Ward, Stokes, and Tucker, p. 36.
27. *The Rolling Stone Interviews*, p. 285.
28. Nick Kent, *The Dark Stuff* (London: Penguin Books, 1994), p. 10.

29. Ibid., p. 12.
30. Ibid., p. 68.
31. Ibid., p. 27.
32. David Walley, *No Commercial Potential: The Story of Frank Zappa and the Mothers of Invention* (New York: Dutton-Sunrise, 1972), p. 26.
33. Ibid., p. 27.
34. Ward, Stokes, and Tucker, p. 336.
35. Lester Bangs, *Rolling Stone*, March 3, 1969, p. 356.

Chapter Six

36. *The Rolling Stone Interviews*, p. 19.
37. *The Rolling Stone Interviews*, p. 227.
38. David Henderson, *'Scuse Me While I Kiss the Sky: The Life of Jimi Hendrix* (New York: Bantam Books, 1978), pp. 189–90.

Chapter 7

39. Bangs, p. 72.
40. Ward, Stokes, and Tucker, p. 452.
41. Ibid., p. 572.
42. Marcus, p. 40.
43. Robert Christgau, *Christgau's Record Guide: Rock Albums of the '70s* (New York: Ticknor and Fields, 1981), p. 117.

Chapter Nine

44. Ward, Stokes, and Tucker, p. 551.
45. Greil Marcus, *Lipstick Traces: A Secret History of the Twentieth Century* (Cambridge: Harvard University Press, 1989), p. 49.
46. Ward, Stokes, and Tucker, p. 534.

Chapter Ten

47. Jon Savage, *England's Dreaming: Anarchy, Sex Pistols, Punk Rock, and Beyond* (New York: St. Martin's Press, 1992), p. 122.
48. Ibid., p. 239.

Chapter Eleven

49. Greil Marcus, *Ranters and Crowd Pleasers* (New York: Doubleday, 1993), p. 100.
50. Christopher Anderson, *Madonna: Unauthorized* (New York: Simon and Schuster, 1991), p. 218.
51. Ibid., p. 269.
52. Ibid., p. 334.
53. Christopher Anderson, *Michael Jackson: Unauthorized* (New York: Simon and Schuster, 1994), p. 89.

Epilogue

54. Gina Arnold, "Better Dead Than Cool: Punk Philosophers Nirvana," *Option*, January/February 1992, p. 72.

SUGGESTED READING

Bangs, Lester. *Psychotic Reactions and Carburetor Dung* (New York: Vintage Books, 1988).

Booth, Stanley. *Rhythm Oil: A Journey Through the Music of the American South* (New York: Vintage Books, 1991).

DeCurtis, Anthony, and James Henke. *The Rolling Stone Album Guide* (New York: Random House, 1992).

Guralnick, Peter. *Last Train to Memphis* (Boston: Back Bay/Little, Brown, 1994).

Kent, Nick. *The Dark Stuff* (London: Penguin Books, 1994).

Marcus, Greil. *Mystery Train: Images of America in Rock 'n' Roll Music* (New York: Plume Books, 1975).

Palmer, Robert. *Deep Blues* (New York: Viking, 1981).

Savage, Jon. *England's Dreaming: Anarchy, Sex Pistols, Punk Rock and Beyond* (New York: St. Martin's Press, 1992).

Tosches, Nick. *Country: The Twisted Roots of Rock 'n' Roll* (New York: Da Capo Press, 1996).

Ward, Ed, Geoffrey Stokes, and Ken Tucker. *Rock of Ages: the Rolling Stone History of Rock & Roll* (New York: Rolling Stone Press, 1986).

SUGGESTED LISTENING

Band, the

Big Pink (Capitol, 1968)
The Band (Capitol, 1969)
Rock of Ages (Capitol, 1972)

Beach Boys, the

Pet Sounds (Capitol, 1990)

Beatles, the

Revolver (Capitol, 1987)
Rubber Soul (Capitol, 1987)
Sgt. Pepper's Lonely Hearts Club Band (Capitol, 1967)
Abbey Road (Apple, 1969)

Beck

Odelay (DGC, 1996)

Berry, Chuck

The Great Twenty-Eight (Chess/MCA, 1984)

Big Star
Radio City (Ardent, 1974)
Sister Lovers (Rykodisc, 1992)

Blood, Sweat and Tears
The Child Is Father to the Man (Columbia, 1968)

Bowie, David
Hunky Dory (Rykodisc, 1990)
The Rise and Fall of Ziggy Stardust and the Spiders from Mars (Rykodisk, 1990)
Station to Station (Rykodisc, 1990)

Buffalo Springfield
Buffalo Springfield (Atco, 1973)

Brown, James
20 All-Time Greatest Hits! (Polydor, 1991)

Byrds, the
Byrds' Greatest Hits (Columbia, 1967)

Captain Beefheart
Safe as Milk (Buddha, 1985)
Trout Mask Replica (Reprise, 1970)

Charles, Ray
Anthology (Rhino, 1989)

Clash, the
Clash (Epic, 1977)
London Calling (Epic, 1979)

Costello, Elvis

My Aim Is True (Columbia, 1977)
This Year's Model (Columbia, 1978)

Cream

Wheels of Fire (Polydor, 1968)
Strange Brew: *The Best of Cream* (Polydor, 1983)

Creedence Clearwater Revival

Chronicle (Fantasy, 1976)

Delaney and Bonnie

On Tour: With Eric Clapton (Atco, 1970)

Derek and the Dominoes

Layla (RSO, 1970)

Diddley, Bo

The Chess Box (Chess/MCA, 1990)

Domino, Fats

They Call Me the Fat Man (EMI, 1991)

Doors, the

Morrison Hotel (Elektra, 1970)

Dylan, Bob

Bringing It All Back Home (Columbia, 1965)
Highway 61 Revisited (Columbia, 1965)
Blonde on Blonde (Columbia, 1966)
Blood on the Tracks (Columbia, 1975)

Eno, Brian

Another Green World (EG Records, 1975)
Before and After Science (EG Records, 1977)

Everly Brothers, the

Cadence Classics (Rhino, 1985)

Fairport Convention

Fairport Chronicles (A&M, 1974)

Franklin, Aretha

30 Greatest Hits (Atlantic, 1985)

Funkadelic

One Nation Under a Groove (Warner Bros.,1978)

Gabriel, Peter

So (Geffen, 1984)

Grateful Dead, the

Workingman's Dead (Warner Bros., 1970)
American Beauty (Warner Bros., 1970)

Harvey, P.J.

To Send You My Love (Island, 1995)

Hendrix, Jimi

Are You Experienced? (Reprise, 1967)
Electric Ladyland (Reprise, 1968)
Smash Hits (Reprise, 1969)

Holly, Buddy
20 Golden Greats (MCA, 1978)

Husker Du
Zen Arcade (SST, 1984)
Candy Apple Grey (Warner Bros., 1986)
Warehouse: Songs and Stories (Warner Bros., 1987)

Jefferson Airplane
Volunteers (RCA, 1969)

John, Elton
Honky Chateau (MCA, 1972)

Joplin, Janis
Pearl (Columbia, 1971)

King, Carole
Tapestry (Ode, 1971)

Kinks, the
Kink Kronikles (Reprise, 1972)

Led Zeppelin
Untitled (Atlantic, 1971)
Houses of the Holy (Atlantic, 1973)

Lennon, John
Plastic Ono Band (Apple/Capitol, 1970)
Imagine (Apple/Capitol, 1970)

Lewis, Jerry Lee
18 Original Sun Greatest Hits (Rhino, 1984)

Little Richard
18 Greatest Hits (Rhino, 1985)
The Specialty Sessions (Specialty, 1990)

Modern Lovers, the
The Modern Lovers (Rhino, 1986)

Morrison, Van
Astral Weeks (Warner Bros., 1968)
Moondance (Warner Bros., 1970)

Nelson, Rick
The Best of Rick Nelson (EMI, 1987)
The Best of Rick Nelson, Vol. 2 (EMI, 1991)

Newman, Randy
12 Songs (Reprise, 1970)
Sail Away (Sail Away, 1972)

New York Dolls, the
Too Much Too Soon (Mercury, 1988)

Nirvana
Nevermind (DGC, 1991)

Orbison, Roy
For the Lonely: A Roy Orbison Anthology, 1956–1964
(Rhino, 1988)

Pere Ubu
Dub Housing (Chrysalis, 1978)

Perkins, Carl
Original Sun Greatest Hits (Rhino, 1986)

Phair, Liz
Exile in Guyville (Matador, 1993)

Pink Floyd
Piper at the Gates of Dawn (Capitol, 1967)
Dark Side of the Moon (Capitol, 1973)

Prefab Sprout
Two Wheels Good (Epic, 1985)

Presley, Elvis
Essential Elvis (RCA, 1988)

Prince
Purple Rain (Warner Bros., 1984)

Public Enemy
It Takes a Nation of Millions to Hold Us Back (Def Jam, 1988)
Fear of a Black Planet (Def Jam, 1990)

Ramones, the
Rocket to Russia (Sire, 1977)

Rascals, the
Time Piece (Atlantic, 1968)

R.E.M.
Murmur (IRS, 1983)
Out of Time (Warner Bros., 1991)

Replacements, the
Let It Be (Twin/Tone, 1984)
Pleased to Meet Me (Sire, 1987)

Rolling Stones, the
The Rolling Stones, Now! (Abkco, 1986)
Beggars Banquet (Abkco, 1986)
Let It Bleed (Abkco, 1986)
Exile on Main Street (Rolling Stones, 1972)

Roxy Music
Stranded (Reprise, 1989)
Siren (Reprise, 1989)
Avalon (Warner Bros., 1982)

Sex Pistols, the
Never Mind the Bollocks (Warner Bros., 1977)

Simon, Paul
Graceland (Warner Bros., 1986)

Sly and the Family Stone
Greatest Hits (Epic, 1970)
There's a Riot Going On (Epic, 1971)

Sonic Youth
Daydream Nation (Enigma/Blast First, 1988)

Springsteen, Bruce
The Wild, the Innocent and the E Street Shuffle (Columbia, 1973)
Born to Run (Columbia, 1975)

Steely Dan
Pretzel Logic (MCA, 1974)

Stewart, Rod
Every Picture Tells a Story (Mercury, 1971)

Stooges, the
Fun House (Elektra, 1970)

Talking Heads
More Songs About Buildings and Food (Sire, 1978)
Remain in Light (Sire, 1980)

Taylor, James
Sweet Baby James (Warner Bros., 1970)

Various Artists
Saturday Night Fever (RSO, 1977)

Velvet Underground
The Velvet Underground and Nico (Verve/Polygram, 1985)
The Velvet Underground (Verve/Polygram, 1985)
Loaded (Cotillion, 1970)

Who, the

The Who Lives at Leeds (MCA, 1970)
Who's Next (MCA, 1971)

Young, Neil

After the Gold Rush (Reprise, 1970)
Tonight's the Night (Reprise, 1975)
Decade (Reprise, 1976)
Rust Never Sleeps (Reprise, 1979)

Zappa, Frank

Freak Out (Rykodisc, 1985)
We're Only in It for the Money (Verve, 1967)
Hot Rats (Rykodisc, 1987)

Appendix
ROCK-AND-ROLL HALL OF FAME
INDUCTEES: 1986-2000

The Rock-and-Roll Hall of Fame opened its ultramodern facilities in Cleveland, Ohio, in 1995. Using a panel of performers, producers, record executives, broadcasters, and music journalists, the organization has been selecting a prestigious group of members since 1986. Along with the seminal rock-and-roll performers of the past 40 years, inductees to the Hall of Fame include country, blues, jazz, and rhythm-and-blues musicians who have had an impact on rock and roll, as well as record executives, songwriters, producers, and disc jockeys who have played a significant role in the music's development.

Following is a list of the Hall of Fame's membership to date, with inductees listed according to the year they were selected:

1986

Chuck Berry

James Brown

Ray Charles

Sam Cooke

Fats Domino

the Everly Brothers

Buddy Holly

Jerry Lee Lewis

Little Richard

Elvis Presley

1987

the Coasters	Rick Nelson
Eddie Cochrane	Roy Orbison
Bo Diddley	Carl Perkins
Ahmet Ertegun	Smokey Robinson
Aretha Franklin	Mike Stoller
Marvin Gaye	Big Joe Turner
Bill Haley	Muddy Waters
Louis Jordan	Jerry Wexler
B. B. King	Hank Williams
Jerry Lieber	Jackie Wilson
Clyde McPhatter	

1988

the Beach Boys	Leadbelly
the Beatles	Les Paul
the Drifters	the Supremes
Bob Dylan	Woody Guthrie
Berry Gordy	

1989

Dion DiMucci	the Soul Stirrers
the Ink Spots	Phil Spector
Otis Redding	the Temptations
the Rolling Stones	Stevie Wonder
Bessie Smith	

1990

Hank Ballard
Bobby Darin
Lamont Dozier
the Four Seasons
the Four Tops
Gerry Goffin
Brian Holland

Eddie Holland
Carole King
the Kinks
the Platters
Simon and Garfunkel
the Who

1991

LaVern Baker
Dave Bartholomew
Ralph Bass
the Byrds
John Lee Hooker

the Impressions
Wilson Pickett
Jimmy Reed
Howlin' Wolf

1992

Bobby (Blue) Bland
Booker T and the MGs
Johnny Cash
the Isley Brothers

the Jimi Hendrix Experience
Sam and Dave
the Staple Singers
the Yardbirds

1993

Ruth Brown
Dick Clark
Cream
Creedence Clearwater Revival
the Doors
Milt Gabler

Billie Holliday
Etta James
Frankie Lymon and the Teenagers
Van Morrison
Sly and the Family Stone
Dinah Washington

1994

Willie Dixon
the Grateful Dead
Elton John
John Lennon

Bob Marley
Johnny Otis
Rod Stewart

1995

Paul Ackerman
the Allman Brothers Band
Al Green
Janis Joplin
Led Zeppelin

Martha (Reeves) and the Vandellas
the Orioles
Neil Young
Frank Zappa

1996

David Bowie
Tom Donahue
Little Willie John
Pink Floyd
the Shirelles

Gladys Knight and the Pips
Jefferson Airplane
Pete Seeger
the Velvet Underground

1997

the (Young) Rascals
the Bee Gees
Buffalo Springfield
Crosby, Stills and Nash

the Jackson Five
Joni Mitchell
Parliament-Funkadelic

1998

the Eagles
Fleetwood Mac
the Mamas and the Papas

Lloyd Price
Santana
Gene Vincent

1999

Billy Joel
Curtis Mayfield
Paul McCartney
Del Shannon

Dusty Springfield
Bruce Springsteen
the Staple Singers

2000

Eric Clapton
Earth, Wind & Fire
Lovin' Spoonful

the Moonglows
Bonnie Raitt
James Taylor

INDEX

ABOUT THE AUTHOR

David Shirley has written many books for children and young adults, including *Everyday I Sing the Blues: The Story of B. B. King.* His writings on popular music have appeared in *Option, Rolling Stone, Chicago Review, Raygun,* and *New York Press.* He lives in Brooklyn, New York.